D1624568

THE REAL SCORE

At Pauma Valley, October 1973
(Photo for Aldila by Coakley Heagerty, Inc.)

THE
REAL SCORE

GENE LITTLER

WITH
JACK TOBIN

Word Books, Publisher . Waco, Texas

To those dearest to me—
  Shirley, my wife,
  Curt, my son,
  Suzanne, my daughter,
  who have shared in my adversities
  and my triumphs and who have
  each made life so worth living

Preface

My fellow professional golfers who have marched beside me over the years on tour may be shocked to find me turned author. I'm afraid that I am known in the world of golf as a man of few words and a little difficult for the golf writers to interview.

No doubt that is partly of my making. But I set these words down because I am convinced there are hundreds, maybe thousands, in the world today who may receive some bit of encouragement to carry on in the face of adversity. We all read about it but seldom realize its full impact until it knocks at our particular door.

It knocked on mine early in 1972. When it was introduced I was shocked, stunned, terrified and fearful.

I had cancer.

Almost immediately the medical experts who were consulted said radical surgery was necessary in the area under my left arm.

When the rest of my fellow professionals were playing in the Masters at Augusta, Georgia, in April 1972, I was admitted to Mercy Hospital in San Diego for surgery that might save my life, might leave me unable to play the game that was my life and livelihood but, most important, might possibly deprive me of being with those I love so dearly—my family.

One seldom sees an instant replay of his life. But the day Dr. Roger Isenhour told me of his fears literally every moment of my life flashed past. Those fears were confirmed by an extensive battery of tests over the next few days.

It was immediately obvious to me that the most important thing in life was my immediate family.

Golf I could do without, either as a professional or a weekend player. But I told the Lord I didn't want to close out my score when my children were so young and my family so vital.

It is doubtful that I decided then and there to tell the world of the fears and tribulations of a cancer victim. But as letter after letter, call after call, telegram after telegram reached me in the hospital or my home in La Jolla, there seemed only one proper and possible response to each.

Thus, this book.

Religion has always been my close partner. It is even closer today. It held me together through the shattering diagnosis, the trauma of surgery, and the tedious recovery.

I want people today and tomorrow who are suddenly faced with that frightening word *cancer* to know that all hope is not lost. There are many thousands of highly skilled, highly trained medical men who are able to turn around your worst fears.

My experience is an example. I do play golf. I do play it professionally. I do win. I do make a fine living in one of the most competitive fields there is. And hopefully, with God's continued assistance, I will be able to be with my family and in my chosen endeavor for many more years.

To those of you who are confronted with a similar challenge there may be some solace, some guidance, some assistance in these pages in your personal hour of tragedy.

It is solely for this reason that I decided to lay out my life and especially those months since my first knowledge that I had cancer.

To those stricken . . . to those who walk beside them . . . may you find comfort here as you face your greatest hour.

1

O⬛O⬛O⬛O⬛O⬛O⬛O⬛

I stood on the eighteenth green at the Norwood Hills Country Club on a hot, humid, almost stifling Sunday afternoon in St. Louis. A curling eight-foot putt had just dropped to close out a string of eleven consecutive pars, and the championship of the St. Louis Classic was mine.

To many it wouldn't mean very much. The St. Louis Classic was just one of the many weekly stops on the 1973 gold trail that spreads from shore to shore and border to border.

It wasn't the U.S. Open. It wasn't the Professional Golfer's Association championship. It wasn't the British Open. It wasn't the Masters.

To me, however, it was the most imposing triumph at a time when a win was vital.

There had been great moments in my life as a golfer. Winning the U.S. Amateur in 1953 at Oklahoma City. Beating a fine field of professionals like Jimmy Demaret, Lloyd Mangrum, Julius Boros and Dr. Cary Middlecoff in the San Diego Open just the week before turning pro in 1954. Those three successive Tournaments of Champions in Las Vegas in 1955, 1956, and 1957. And winning what many consider the highest honor in American golf—the U.S. Open title in 1961.

9

They were all special—moments you cherish throughout your career. But standing on that sprawling green at Norwood with the whistles, cheers, and applause ringing round, I had all I could do to keep from breaking into tears when my eight-footer plopped in the cup.

I was back.

I'd made it back to the tour.

Now I'd made it back to the top of the pack.

I'd won a major tournament against some of the finest professionals in the world.

Maybe it wasn't the U.S. Open, nor the British, nor the PGA, nor the Masters. But I was back, and the St. Louis Classic was a most appropriate tournament in which to record my first triumph since May 23, 1971, when I won the Colonial National Invitational on Ben Hogan's favorite course in Fort Worth, Texas.

Just fifteen months and nineteen days back—April 4, 1972, to be precise—I had undergone cancer surgery which had literally wiped out the essential muscle structure on my left arm and side. I was then just willing to settle for living and let golf go by the wayside.

But I was back.

Officially, the tournament was the St. Louis Children's Hospital Classic. A more apropos title could not have been conceived for me. It was only the second year the tournament had been played. I won it on the final hole with a 68 and a 268 total. What was more important, throughout that blistering day I staved off repeated challenges from Bruce Crampton and Lee Trevino (who made up our threesome) as well as Bert Yancey and Bob Goalby.

I recall the press room on that July day in 1973 and the gauntlet of writers who were trying to put into words my immediate feelings on the moment. The good Lord had been kind to me. He'd answered my innumerable prayers to live with my family and tossed in golf as a bonus.

"I don't know how to describe my feelings," I told the media representatives assembled in the press room. "It's the greatest personal thrill I have ever had in golf." I continued thinking back to the days and weeks when playing tournament golf appeared very doubtful and winning impossible.

"Does that include the U.S. Open?" one of the writers asked. The impact of my one-stroke victory over Crampton began to assume even greater proportions than it had when that last putt dropped in.

My mind was still cluttered by the roar of the gallery, the immediate congratulations of Trevino, Crampton, and my other friends on the tour, plus those of the hundreds of well-wishers. Their faces were hardly recognizable as I moved slowly toward the press room after the presentation ceremony.

"Does that include the U.S. Open?" I asked myself, pulling myself back to the reality of the interview.

Sixteen months ago there would not have been a moment's hesitation. The Open was my biggest moment of triumph—but that was before April 4, 1972.

Now it was another matter and there was really only the question of a reply. In those fleeting seconds I wondered to myself where Shirley and Curt and Suzy were when that putt dropped.

Had they seen it? What was my answer?

"Winning the U.S. Open was a thrill, of course," I readily admitted, "but when you do something you believed you'd never do again . . . that's got to be a great thrill.

"As much as the Open. . . . Maybe even more than the Open.

"A year ago," I frankly confessed, "I didn't know if I'd ever play golf again or if I'd ever be able to be a competitive tour golfer again—let alone win."

I guess when it's your turn to win, you just win.

Even on Wednesday after the Pro-Am there was a grave question in my mind whether I'd ever play in the St. Louis tournament proper. Shortly after completing my round in the Pro-Am, I began to have severe stomach pains and finally cramps. My son, Curt, who was along with me as well as my wife, Shirley, and my daughter, Suzanne, insisted I go to the hospital.

A few years before when Curt had similar pains and we kept putting it off, he ended up with a ruptured appendix. This time we went to a nearby emergency hospital where a doctor examined me at great length. He didn't believe it was my appendix nor any major problem. Rather he thought it was probably an upset stomach from food poisoning or something like a 24-hour virus.

We stayed in the hospital for several hours, leaving near midnight for our motel. By the next morning I felt a little better, at least well enough to tee off at my regular starting time.

Whatever the ailment, it didn't bother my game. I shot a 66, one stroke back of Rik Massengale and Goalby, who both had 65s. The next day I came back with another 66 to take the halfway lead with 8 under par, 132. Then back-to-back scores of 68 gave me the winning 268 total and a hefty first-prize check of $42,000, considerably more than the $36,941 I had earned in fifteen previous tournament appearances in 1973.

It's the kind of a triumph you like in a year that had not begun too impressively. In one of my all-time favorites—the Los Angeles Open—I had finished 41st. The $472 I earned there hardly paid my caddy fees, let alone entry fee, motel bills, meals, and other expenses.

Three weeks later it was even worse in one of the great tests of golf—the Bing Crosby National Pro-Amateur, where I finished 61st in the field, 17 strokes back of Jack Nicklaus's winning 290, and earned only $337.50.

I was thinking about those finishes when I started the final round in St. Louis on that torrid Sunday. Trevino led after three rounds with an 11-under 199. A stroke back, I was wondering how to survive and win in what I knew would be a testing final round. The heat was simply oppressive. It was hot just to breathe, and the air was almost stifling.

As we played our way around I took every opportunity to rest, to relax, and especially to get into any shade, even that created by the gallery. One of the photographs showed me sitting on the butt end of my golf bag as Trevino was lining up a putt. My chin was resting on my closed fist, and people asked me what I was thinking about. All I can recall was trying to be a bit cool.

We were back and forth throughout the last eighteen. First

it was Trevino ahead, then Crampton, then me. Bruce, who is especially tough in head-to-head play, was two strokes back of me when we went to the 17th, where he missed the green. He had a tough chip that had to be hit just right to get it anywhere near the flag. But he made a perfect shot and holed it out.

Now I was up by a stroke with the 18th to play. Bruce is a tremendous competitor and is especially good when the going gets tough.

My drive kind of popped up. My second shot wasn't one you would brag about. It was slightly fat and came up a bit short of the green. My chip was a bit strong too and left me about an eight-footer for a par that would win or a bogey for a tie. Bruce had two-putted from about eighteen to twenty feet away for a 67.

When I stood over my ball carefully examining the break of the green, the pressure of that one shot, that one putt, suddenly became awesome within me. If ever a man needed help from above it was me. When I tapped the ball and it began its little curl I knew everything was right except the break. But it plopped into the cup with the sweetest sound I'd ever heard.

It was my twenty-fifth tour win but one with tremendous personal meaning. The previous twenty-four were all important but, looking back, that final day in St. Louis and that final putt to win gave me something I will remember forever.

2

○◼○◼○◼○◼○◼○◼○◼○◼

Certain days seem to stand out indelibly. Thursday, March 9, 1972, for instance. It was the week after the Doral-Eastern Open in Miami. I was back home in La Jolla basking in the California sun, puttering with my antique cars, getting some practice in so I could pick up the tour at the Greater Greensboro Open at Sedgefield Country Club in Greensboro, North Carolina, just before the Masters in Augusta.

It was a beautiful March day and I had spent a good part of it at my home club, the La Jolla Country Club, working on the fine points of my game. I had come home a bit earlier than usual because I had an appointment for my annual physical examination with Dr. Roger C. Isenhour, an internist who had been my dad's physician for many years. I had been seeing him annually for a checkup for a half dozen years.

In his office we joshed around as usual, talking about a lot of things—my golf game, the antique car collection, the kids, my wife, the house—everything a patient and his doctor might discuss.

It was what I'd call easy conversation. All the time he was going about giving me a physical—height, weight, measurements, the routine most of us go through every year or two. He

14

was feeling around my chest, thumping here and there as doctors do while they listen to their stethoscopes.

Then he had me raise my arms. Suddenly I realized he was pushing awfully hard under my left armpit. He seemed to spend an extra long time in that area. Then he moved over under the other arm. Then back to the left arm again.

"I don't like that," I remember him telling me.

"Here," he said, taking my right hand and pushing it deeply into the spot he had been probing under my left armpit, "can you feel that?"

"Feel what?" I asked. "I don't feel a thing."

He explained that deep in the recess of the armpit there appeared to be a growth. He wasn't sure of its size or just what it meant, but obviously he was quite concerned.

By coincidence, later that afternoon I had an appointment with another doctor who was able to find the same lump when I told him. He agreed that it should be watched carefully for a period.

The next day, after not a very good night's sleep nor a very good practice session at La Jolla Country Club, I went back to Dr. Isenhour again.

With a night to think about it he was much more emphatic. "No, I don't want to wait. We've got to have this looked at by a totally independent surgeon."

He called Dr. James Higgins, a surgeon in the same building, and we both went down to see him. After Dr. Higgins had punched around for awhile he told us it was his opinion that I should have it checked out immediately—with a surgical biopsy.

They arranged for me to enter Donald Sharp Memorial Hospital in San Diego on an in-patient–out-patient basis March 15. Dr. Higgins, assisted by Dr. Edward Person, did the biopsy. By late afternoon I was out of Sharp Memorial with little pain and not too much concern.

Three days later I was out practicing at La Jolla, readying my game for the Masters the first week in April, when I got a phone call from Dr. Isenhour.

"I've got bad news for you," he told me after a bit of our

usual amiable conversation. "The biopsy shows the growth is malignant."

It was like a sledge hammer falling on me.

Cancer.

That was something I'd heard about from time to time, but it never dawned on me that I would be a target. We take things for granted in this world. That cancer will never hit us.

But it had hit me.

Cancer.

A terrifying word at that time. It stood for one thing to me—death.

I spent the rest of the day having tests. There was no way I could continue playing golf. The Masters coming up was important. But compared to what faced me—cancer surgery—it was nothing.

When I walked in Shirley knew something was wrong. She can read me like no golfer can a green. We sat down. I told her the findings. The prognosis. That Dr. Isenhour and the other surgeons felt it had been discovered very early and properly diagnosed. That it wasn't all dark. That there was great hope. We talked the afternoon out.

After dinner we had a little family meeting around the oval table in our den, where you can hear the roar of the Pacific Ocean when the sliding door is open. We told Curt, who had just turned eighteen on March 11, and Suzanne, who was then fourteen.

It was a traumatic experience.

Dr. Isenhour was a kindly man in the situation. He took a great deal of time to explain the full import of the diagnosis, the various options in surgery, but, most important, that cancer didn't necessarily mean instant death.

He was willing to postpone surgery until after the Masters. The tournament was scheduled for April 6–9 in Augusta.

"Let's do what you feel we should do now," I told him.

"Golf is important to me, but this is a lot more important. I don't care if I play again if I live. Let's do it and get it over with."

Dr. Isenhour assured me again and again that postponing

the operation two weeks or so would not create a major problem.

"There's no way I can play golf competitively," I told him. "It would be impossible for me to concentrate. I might concentrate for a drive, but all I'd be thinking about walking down the fairway to my second shot was if the surgery would be a success.

"It has to be done . . . and now."

We tentatively set surgery for April 4 at Mercy Hospital in San Diego. In between I consulted with practically every medical man in San Diego about the proposed surgical process.

Dr. Isenhour insisted that I fly to New York to consult one of the leading specialists in melanomas, Dr. Lemuel Bowden of the Memorial Sloan-Kettering Cancer Center in New York City.

With all my diagnostic material in hand, I flew to New York City for my appointment with Dr. Bowden. He confirmed the procedure proposed by the surgeons and its urgency.

It was a long, lonely plane ride home. Now, however, I had checked all the alternatives two or three times. The opinion was unanimous—surgery.

As it was explained to me, Dr. Harvey P. Groesbeck, the surgeon selected to do the work, would make a dissection of the upper left axillary. That meant they would go up under my arm and take out all the lymph nodes plus whatever surrounding muscle tissue, nerves, and anything else were imperative to recovery. It would be a surgical process known as a "one-piece envelope" in which they would make the incision or incisions so as to take all the potentially cancerous tissue in one large envelope.

Dr. Groesbeck was so great in explaining everything in a very encouraging way and in language we could understand. He is a great surgeon and a fine man, with a quality about him that gives you the certain assurance that everything is going to come out all right.

Once I was back from New York, we firmed up April 4 as the date for surgery. There was no sense in delaying. I couldn't think of much else. I didn't sleep well, sometimes hardly at all.

Golf was impossible to keep my mind on, although I played a little and even practiced some.

About the only place I could forget about the upcoming event was out in the garage working on my 1959 Rolls Royce I was restoring, or tinkering with Curt's 1955 Thunderbird.

Cancer was still a terrifying word to me although I spent a great deal of my time learning more and more about it.

My immediate reaction after that call from Dr. Isenhour was probably the same as most.

"Gee, how long have I got to live?"

3

Between my return from New York and the date of surgery, I spent a great deal of time reading. Dr. Isenhour, Dr. Groesbeck, and my friend Dave Freeman, once the world's best badminton player and now a highly successful neurosurgeon in San Diego, guided me to numerous books and articles on melanoma-type cancer.

They were written so an average guy like me could understand the problem and the potential. By the surgery date, I was far less terrified than I had been when Dr. Isenhour dropped his bomb on me. I was pretty well convinced that if they were able to get it all I had a good chance of living.

That was a whole lot more than I believed two weeks earlier when I got the word of the malignancy.

The morning of April 3, 1972, rolled around quickly. There wasn't much packing to be done—a razor, toothbrush and paste, a robe and some slippers—and me.

We—Shirley and the kids and I—all got into the Rolls I was slowly restoring and began our little drive from La Jolla to downtown San Diego. I checked in about 4:00 P.M. and was assigned to room 1131. Sister Placida, the executive director, practically took me in hand to guide me through all the admission procedures.

When I arrived at Mercy I was a little stunned. Hanging from the steel girders on a new addition was a huge sign. "GOOD LUCK, GENE," it said. After reading in the paper I was going into Mercy that day, the hard hats working up there in the sky had the sign made and hung out for me. That banner gave me quite a lift as I walked into the hospital, a sign from a bunch of guys I'd never met and probably would never see again. They sure made me feel good. They cared.

It was pretty tough going. I knew the surgeons were going to do a radical process. That could mean I'd come out with a good prognosis to live but not much hope to play golf again. As I said, I'd be willing to settle for life. But you always like to push your luck a bit and I'm no exception.

Deep down I wanted to play golf again, if not on the tour, at least for fun. I loved the game either way.

A radical dissection of the left axillary didn't hold much hope for golf. Literally all the muscle in the area completely under my left arm along the side of my chest and into my back would be gone.

Everyone who plays golf has always heard it called a left-sided game. I didn't think there'd be enough left of me on that side to play a midget golf course at the arcade, let alone take a whack at Augusta or Pebble Beach.

That Monday afternoon they gave me more tests, took more blood samples, checked more things than I ever believed possible. When they shaved me skin-clean all above my waist on the left side, the total impact of just what was going to be involved became graphically clear. They were going to do a lot of cutting on Gene boy.

By evening time all the prep work—as the nurses called it—was over. All the doctors had been in to see me. Dr. Isenhour, Dr. Groesbeck, the anesthetists—a regular parade—and even Sister Placida. This was one Lutheran sure getting a lot of attention in a Roman Catholic hospital.

Surgery was scheduled for Tuesday at 8:00 A.M. We watched TV and talked through most of the evening before Shirley and the kids went home. They gave me a sleeping pill—something I normally avoid—but if I hadn't had it I don't think I'd have slept much.

The next thing I knew the nurses were awakening me for surgery. I gave Shirley a call since she's an early riser also, and the wait began. By the time Shirley got to the hospital I was pretty sedated but not out.

Eight o'clock came and went and there was no one rolling me down to surgery. Our pastor, Quentin Garman, arrived moments after Shirley and spent the whole day waiting with me, which meant a lot. We received delay after delay. One emergency after another kept pushing my spot on the schedule farther and farther back.

I don't really recall much about that day except the delay. They tried to keep me sedated but I insisted on getting up and walking around the room. Shirley tells me I was a happy-go-lucky, easy-going guy all that day as they tried to keep me relaxed. Though I was supposed to stay in bed, I was out more than in and prowling around the room in what you wouldn't call steady fashion. In fact, Curt said I'd never pass a heel and toe test if a cop had come in the room.

We finally beat the schedule but it was about 7:30 P.M. instead of 8:00 A.M. I really don't remember being rolled off to surgery as they gave me a shot a half hour or so before time. Shirley tells me I came out of surgery about 9:30 P.M. but my first recollection was the next morning when I woke up.

I must have felt pretty good because I had no problem remembering our number when I called Shirley about 6:15. There have been times when I have forgotten it, especially if we have just changed it—a necessity from time to time. No matter how you limit an unlisted number, pretty soon it's all over and you have to change.

I never realized that a golfer's operation could be so important. The phone never quit at home and the hospital had to put out news bulletins for the media. They even gave me a copy. The first one said:

"For immediate release: 8:45 P.M., Tuesday, April 4, 1972.

"A spokesman from the Department of Surgery at Mercy

Hospital and Medical Center stated that this evening Gene Littler underwent cancer surgery at Mercy Hospital, San Diego, California.

"The operation, termed 'left axillary dissection,' consisted of removing all the gland-bearing tissue beneath the left arm and lasted approximately two hours.

"Gene tolerated the procedure well and his post-operative condition is satisfactory.

"The tissue removed at surgery will be analyzed in detail by the laboratory and results of the study should be available by Friday (April 7).

"Another progress report regarding Gene Littler's condition will be made on Wednesday morning (after 10:00 A.M.)."

A number of those bulletins were put out. The Sister Superior told me the phone never quit, that the switchboard was all aglow. I'll never understand why, but I certainly appreciated the interest, letters, telegrams, flowers, and messages that poured in for days and days.

The first thing I really remember was early the next morning. The physical therapist walked in and asked me how I felt. When I told her OK, she said: "Fine. Come on, now; let's move your arm."

I did everything I'd always done to move my left arm but it just continued lying there dead on the bed. I couldn't wiggle a finger.

Panic set in. If the therapist really expected me to be able to move it and nothing would happen, my worst fears were realized. I wouldn't ever play golf. I probably couldn't ever use it again. Not if I couldn't wiggle a finger.

My doctors didn't tell me at the time, but I learned later they didn't give me much hope about playing golf professionally. Living, yes. Golf, no. And looking down at that arm at that moment I had to agree. I never thought I'd hit another ball, at least not as a competitive professional.

My spirits took a big jump on Thursday afternoon. Edward G. Hertfelder, the chief administrator of Mercy Hospital, came in with a piece of paper in his hand and gave it to me.

It was on hospital stationery and was for 5:00 P.M. release to the media, Thursday, April 6, 1972:

"Re: Gene Littler (Report #5)," it read.

"A spokesman from the Department of Surgery at Mercy Hospital and Medical Center said that detailed analysis of the entire tissue removed during his operation on April 4 revealed no remaining cancer."

Wow!

What relief.

I can't possibly describe what an impact that had on me.

Now maybe I really could live.

Then I remembered the therapist coming in that morning and laying a little one-pound dumbbell in my left hand.

"Let's see you raise that up," she said.

Raise it up! I couldn't even grasp it. Couldn't roll it around in my palm. Couldn't even move it.

Imagine. One pound and I couldn't move it. How in the world would I ever hit a golf ball or pound out a ding in a fender?

During surgery it was necessary that a large group of nerves be pulled aside to expose the area where the tumor had been. This resulted in nerve damage—at least that's how my friend Dr. Dave Freeman explained it to me—that prevented me from moving my left arm properly. But I had great confidence in Dave and he insisted it would come back.

I was glad Dave was confident and I sure hoped God was, because the way it looked to me from that tilt-top hospital bed, old Gene Littler's golf days were gone.

4

○■○■○■○■○■○■○■○■

Dave Freeman knew how important golf was to me. He'd been a great athlete in his day, dominating badminton competition in the United States and being a mighty good tennis player. So he knew my problem, how vital therapy was to my recovery, first as a person and second as a golfer.

I'll never forget that little one-pound dumbbell. I couldn't lift it a bit. I'd place my arm on the table and the therapist would wrap my hand around that little hunk of iron and I would strain and strain and strain with everything I could muster and it just lay there.

It seemed mighty ridiculous to a man of my size and my strength not even to be able to wiggle it. But if you don't have any nerve impulse to your muscles, then nothing can happen. All I had was an arm and a hand that couldn't even wrinkle the sheets.

In two or three days after surgery almost all the muscles had atrophied. I could almost see them wither away. It was frightening despite all the words of assurance from Dr. Freeman, Dr. Groesbeck, and the therapist and all the nurses that those nerves would come back in time.

It was like speaking English to a foreign arm. We were unable to communicate on any wavelength I tried. And, man, how I tried.

I got a big boost two or three days after surgery. Shirley was in my room when the door slowly poked open and who should be standing there but Ken Venturi. He had broken a golf date with Frank Sinatra and then-Vice President Spiro Agnew to drive over from Palm Springs to see me, something I greatly appreciated.

"It looks like the rough at the Masters," Ken said, pointing to all the flowers, plants, and cards that had poured in from all over the country. So many flowers came in that I'd have had to leave the bed if we hadn't sent them around to others on the floor.

Ken needled me a bit about the good luck banner that was still flying from the new wing. He insisted that I'd had it painted and hung up there myself. And of course he wouldn't let me convince him I hadn't.

Jack Murphy, the sports editor of the *San Diego Union*, dropped in along with Venturi. Between the two of them they gave me a thorough going over. That was good because it took my mind off the problem of the moment—lifting that one-pound dumbbell.

My doctors told me I was in for several weeks of extensive therapy; that maybe, with luck, in a month or so I could pick up a club and hold it. Maybe in a couple more months I might be able to swing a club without hitting any balls and after that only time would govern my progress.

Several times during that week I thought a lot about where I might have been. It was Masters week and the first round was on Thursday. That's the day I wrestled around so long with that one-pound dumbbell.

I don't know the precise weight of a golf ball but I wondered to myself several times if I could even pick one up. Two years before I remember striding down the fairways at Augusta with a huge crowd following. I was in a playoff with my longtime rival from San Diego, Billy Casper, for the Masters championship. I lost it when I shot a 74 in that eighteen-hole playoff and Billy shot a very solid 69. Now all I would be able to do was watch the 1972 Masters on the tube.

Even if the surgical clamp had not damaged that cluster of nerves I probably couldn't have done too much with that one-pound dumbbell.

I was supposed to spend a full seven days in the hospital after surgery but by Friday I was fit to be tied. I was bugging everyone in sight to release me, especially Dr. Groesbeck, who had to sign me out. Friday evening when he came by on his rounds he asked me if I wanted to go home.

"Now?" I asked, almost leaping out of bed.

"Now" would have to wait until tomorrow but I could be released on Saturday—four days after surgery—if I promised to go home, take it easy, and follow the involved therapy schedule outlined for me.

Saturday morning, April 8, 1972, at almost 11:00 A.M. on the nose, we walked out of Mercy Hospital—"we" meaning the whole family. I don't think I ever enjoyed the drive from San Diego to our home in the highlands of La Jolla more. I'd really like to have been behind the wheel of the car but I had promised the doctors I'd follow the recovery program, and driving, at the moment, wasn't among the list of permitted activities.

There was one person besides myself who must have been glad to see me leave Mercy Hospital—the mail man. I got a ton of mail. What it amounted to was sacks. People from all over the country who had had the same thing wrote me. They all gave me great encouragement. Many were back playing golf and all assured me that I'd be back on the tour as good as ever.

That was great comfort and consolation. Right then I wasn't overly concerned about playing golf. I just wanted to stay around with Shirley, Curt, Suzy, and all my family. I'd settle for just being around a while longer.

I tried to answer all those letters but it became overwhelming. People just wrote to

Gene Littler
La Jolla, California

And while we may spend a lot of time knocking the postal system, those letters reached me at the hospital. And when I went home they came to the house. That's remarkable service.

I carried one little piece of that hospital away with me. That one-pound dumbbell.

I was determined I was going to lift that little beauty, because if I didn't, I wasn't going to lift any golf club or even a ball-peen hammer again.

The doctors lined me up with a therapy schedule that was far more demanding timewise than any practice program I'd ever created myself. Three times a week I had to go to the therapist for treatment including what they called electrical stimulation—I guess you would say it was shocks of electricity to stimulate the muscles in that nerve cluster in my left arm.

About the first of May they told me I could swim. We kicked the thermostat up on our pool and the stronger I got the more often I'd go in—not too long at one time but just enough to try and develop the use of my left arm. For awhile I was a one-armed swimmer.

After several days at home I got so I could lift that one pound. We were using manual-resistance therapy, stretching faithfully each day with Shirley providing the manual resistance. As we stepped up the weight it became more and more difficult for Shirley to keep my arm from wobbling with the correct resistance pressure, so I also rigged a stretching pulley in the garage since the doctors and the therapists all told me the stretching was so vital to recovery.

The first time I realized that my left arm was really coming back was in the pool one early June day. I was kind of meandering easily along in my one-armed style when suddenly I realized that my left arm was doing a little moving. When it was apparent that my arm was actually helping a bit I was ready to do a little leaping around. It's surprising how fast it came back once it started. The pool is forty feet long and I was soon doing twenty to twenty-five laps a session. I tried to get in two a day, sometimes three. The water felt good. It was about 82 degrees and had a definite therapeutic value.

Shirley was like my own private-duty nurse, only she worked a 24-hour shift. No matter where I was she was right there, so

I didn't get by with much. But having been married to me for so many years, she accepted the fact that I was going to create my own little recovery program.

I remember the first morning out of the hospital. Shirley was in making breakfast and I decided that if I could make hospital corners in Navy boot camp I sure could make our bed with just one arm. I was going along pretty good when she caught me. It wasn't the best-looking bed I'd ever seen but it was my biggest accomplishment in nearly a week so I was pretty pleased.

Driving still wasn't permitted. But one day not long after I got home when I was out in the garage puttering around and had to get at something, I found out what I could do with one hand. The car had to be moved, and I wasn't about to go in and ask Shirley. So with my left arm in one of those crazy slings, I got behind the wheel, started up the car, and moved it.

Taking all that therapy became a lot easier on my wife from that point on, since she no longer had to drive me everywhere.

What I really needed was our 1930 Model A Ford that had a rumble seat. One of the tires on the 1924 Rolls Royce was flat. I'd jacked it up with my right hand, got the tire off and somehow put it in the rumble seat so I could go down and get it fixed.

Since hoisting that big tire didn't seem like too much of a problem, I decided to strip the '59 Rolls, sand it down, and paint it. Usually such jobs take me months and months. This one began in April and by the late part of June it was all done. I had taken everything off I could—fenders, doors, hoods, bumpers, all removable parts—leaving just the body intact.

Most of the time I matched the description you've heard of a one-armed paperhanger. I had my left arm in the sling and would stick it inside the waistband of my work pants to keep it out of the way. As time went by and feeling came back, I began to do a little sanding. I used my left hand to hold the paper, and my right hand kind of pushed both hands around.

As I progressed I'd break away from the cars and go with Curt, Shirley, and Suzy up to the tennis courts to play a little, often morning and evening. I was never much of a tennis player but I got pretty good those evenings playing doubles. I'd stick my left arm inside my shirt or in my pants and whale away. It was fun. (Really, every game has to be fun even when it is your business.)

One of the brightest days of my postoperative weeks came the second week or so of June with my brother Jack. He was having trouble with his golf game. He had the shanks and thought a lesson might straighten things out a bit. I kept telling him what he was doing wrong but wasn't getting my point across.

"Here," I told him, "give me that wedge. Let me show you what I mean."

I guess I wasn't really thinking. I just closed my hands around the wedge and swung through. The right hand takes the club back so once you get it going the momentum gets it through the swing arc. I couldn't believe it. I had swung a club when I couldn't even lift an arm by itself. More important, I'd given that ball a good ride.

With that I decided to hit one or two more. We were up at the University of California driving range. I was doing much better than I had earlier with my son. Curt and I had gone out perhaps a week or so before to La Jolla Country Club just to chip some soft shots up to the green, and I couldn't stop shanking the ball. I had no control of my left arm; it was just sort of in the way. Time after time I shanked those chip shots. I seemed to be overpowering things with the right.

But this day with Jack it seemed to come together. That's when I realized that golf was really a right-handed game instead of left-handed as I'd been told since I was old enough to hold a club.

Experts had always told every pupil that it was a left-handed game. It couldn't be. I had no muscle structure on the left side to use. It had to be a right-handed game. Every pro I ever talked with or watched give a lesson always stressed, "Pull through with your left side."

I had a tough time pulling through the water in our pool with my left side so it had to be a guiding situation that the left side produced rather than the primary power force.

Excited . . . I was like a little kid when Jack and I left Cal to go home. It topped even the feelings I'd had a few weeks earlier on a Saturday night just eleven days after surgery. The San Diego Padres asked me to throw out the first ball to open their National League season April 15.

I'd never been on the field in a stadium packed with people and when the cheers began to roll down on me after I was introduced I got a big lump in my throat and that baseball—my first love as a kid—became awfully big and awfully heavy.

Jack Murphy wrote that I "underclubbed it a bit" since the ball bounced a few feet short of the Padres' catcher, Bob Barton. As I walked off the mound the roar of the crowd became even louder. I waved to them all, happy to be there, but most happy just to be alive and able to throw a baseball even if it was only sixty feet or so.

I'd never got beyond playground ball as a kid but the memory of my reception that evening in San Diego Stadium stands out, and I offered up thanks to God that He'd allowed me to walk out there and make that feeble flip to home plate.

5

San Diego's always been my home. And for years I thought Mercy Hospital, where our son Curt was born and where I had surgery, was my birthplace. Whenever I'd drive by, I would say, "That's where I was born—July 21, 1930, at 8:30 A.M."

One day my mother was with me. "Oh, no," she told me. "You weren't born in Mercy. You were born in McCullock Hospital." She should know. I was just chagrined that McCullock Hospital, which was at the east end of San Diego, is no longer operating, so I can't point it out to anybody.

One thing I do know for sure: my given name is Gene. Many insist it is Eugene, but my birth certificate and Mom confirm it is Gene Alec. Sometimes I have as tough a time convincing people of that as Mom did me about the hospital.

I am her third son. My half-brother, Dick Swift, who is head of an electronics firm in Concord, California, is six years older than I am. My other brother, Jack Littler, is two years older. Because of the great difference in Dick's age and mine, Jack and I were much closer as kids. When we were getting old enough to play, Dick was ten or twelve and didn't want much to do with a bunch of little kids.

Although my father was born in England (where he learned

31

to play a little golf as a boy), my parents actually met and were married in South America. My dad's name was Stanley but he went by the name of Fred. He was an accountant, mainly in the construction business, all his life.

That's why he went to South America, in fact. The Guggenheim corporation had world-wide mining interests, especially in Chile, where Dad migrated from London. He worked for a Chilean subsidiary of what was then American Smelting and Refining Company, controlled by the Guggenheim family.

Mom was born in Colorado and came to California when she was about eleven. Her father was a master mechanic, highly skilled in iron work and was quite creative. In her home here in San Diego, Mom still has some of the fancy wrought-iron work he did.

The Guggenheims hired my granddad in Los Angeles and sent him to Chile, where he became ill with inflammatory rheumatism. When the family had to come back to the states, they settled here in San Diego, buying a little mom and pop grocery store. A few years later Mom's parents returned to Chile, and she rejoined them there after Dick was born and she had divorced his father. That's where she met Dad and they were married—in a little town called Tocopilla near Santiago.

After about a year or two in Chile, they decided to come back to San Diego to live. Dad got a job with the R. E. Hazard Construction Company as a bookkeeper, working his way up to be an executive with the firm. He was a vice-president when he passed away.

Dad was awfully close to all of us. From the time I turned pro until his death he handled a great deal of my business affairs. He went over the books that Shirley has always kept, handled a good deal of the business correspondence, and when we were off on tour took care of all the important mail. He made sure everything I became involved in was to my benefit.

One of my earliest recollections is of our first house in old Mission Beach. It was a little old white house that I guess you'd call a California bungalow. I remember it had wood siding. It was near the bay and the ocean, and it was a great place for a 4- or 5-year-old. There was never a problem finding things to do or places to play.

It was fairly close to the main street—Mission Boulevard—and nearby there was a little grocery store where we'd go to buy candy—Jack and some of the kids in the neighborhood, usually. Dick was so much older that he played with an entirely different group.

When I was about six or seven, Dad was doing well enough that he decided to build a house in new Mission Beach right on the bay front. With the ocean a block or two to the west and the bay right at our door, I was pretty much of a beach rat for four or five years. Out in front of the house we had a little pier with a small boat tied up to it. All we had to do was walk out the door and we could almost fall in the water.

I'll never forget learning how to swim. The house was hardly finished when Mom took me to a swimming teacher in Mission Beach. We had our lessons at a little pier going out into the bay. The teacher would tie a rope around your waist and toss you into the water, hanging onto you with a big old bamboo fishing pole. The old rope was a harness and he'd tell you to start flailing away. If you went under he'd just pull you up, sputtering, from the water. The first time he tossed me in I was scared to death. I went down in that water and thought I was never going to come up.

Surprisingly enough, in a few days I could paddle around in the bay with no trouble although my teacher still had that leash on me for security. I sure was scared the first time he took it off, but I didn't sink and the fear vanished very quickly.

From then on it was a ball living on the bay. We learned to body surf over in the open ocean and whenever the waves were good we'd be out riding them. Once in a while in the summer when it was real hot we'd have a wiener bake over by the ocean. A whole raft of kids would bring hot dogs, maybe a potato or two, and we'd cook dinner. I don't know how well things were done but they sure tasted good.

We knew every kid in sight. San Diego, in those days, of course, wasn't a city of nearly a million as it is now. At the beach usually just people in the neighborhood were around—not the thousands we have coming now from other parts of the state and inland to vacation.

Sometimes three or four of us would row out in the bay in our little boat to try our hand at fishing, and once in a while we'd catch something. Jack was a lot better at it than I was. Actually, I never really went much for boating but I never knew why until some years later when I discovered I had a motion sickness problem. Roller coasters, back seats of cars, boats, and even airplanes just weren't for me. Until the jet age arrived, I didn't really like the thought of flying to tournaments.

Not too long ago I was amazed to read in a national magazine that one of my favorite hobbies now was deep sea fishing. That just shows you how facts get distorted. You couldn't get me to go deep sea fishing.

Childhood memories of the beach always bring to mind a man I remember with great fondness. His name was Bill Shewbert and he was grounds superintendent at Mission Beach Elementary School as long as I was around. He simply loved kids. He had children of his own, a daughter and two sons, so he understood our problems. Besides being custodian of the school, he was a Boy Scoutmaster. Later on he became a San Diego policeman but when I knew him we thought he ran the school. In fact, we really thought he was the coach because he was always out on the playground with us getting games going and teaching us how to play baseball, softball, basketball—all the games you learn to play in elementary school. During the summer and evenings when it was warm he'd be out on the beach playing with us. Today you'd call him a recreation director because that's what he did—direct the kids how to play and how to get along.

We were up at his house a lot and I remember his wife used to give kids haircuts. She was better than the barber and you couldn't beat the price—free.

Although I admired Bill as if he were a big brother, my interest in Scouting just barely got me past the Tenderfoot stage. Jack, who cared more about it, and I did go to Scout camp together one year. The only thing I can remember about it is that I didn't go for sleeping out on the ground and after about two days was ready to go home.

Much as I liked the beach and swimming and surfing, though, there was something I liked even more—baseball. I adored it. In the summer when school was out Mom could find me as often as not at the school grounds playing baseball. If we didn't have enough for a five- or six-man team, we'd play over the line with two or three to a side. Bill was the one who taught us to play over the line. He used to kid me about being the best at it. I guess I wasn't too bad. I could always hit the ball fairly long and maybe all that power could have been used on a baseball field. I enjoyed the action you got at short; I was quick enough to play a pretty good game there, and I could get most of the balls hit my way.

There was even a time when my ambition was to be the shortstop of the old San Diego Padres team that played in the Pacific Coast League. Dad used to take us to their games back when the field was right at the ocean front near all the fishing boats. That was a great park for a kid. I don't remember how much the game cost but you could have a whale of a day for a dollar.

Somewhere in an article about me a writer commented that there were several things I could have been besides a professional golfer. He named baseball player, as well as wrestler, mechanic, violinist, and carpenter. Mechanic and carpenter . . . that could have been, maybe even baseball. But the other two . . . I doubt very seriously.

Wrestling was just something Jack and I always seemed to be doing around the house. Mom was always running us out. I remember one day we were thrashing around when she'd gone to the store and somehow we knocked one of those little flimsy slats out of the venetian blinds. We thought we got it back in pretty well so Mom would never notice it but I'll be darned if she didn't catch it within five minutes after she got home.

Violin was something I began, not by choice (I don't think), but more by request. My folks told me to.

There was quite a bit of music interest in the family. My

mom played the accordion. My oldest brother, Dick, played piano and he's still pretty good on one. Jack played trumpet and my dad played the cello.

With all those instruments to buy there wasn't much money around to buy anything for me. I think I wanted to try the clarinet but I ended up with the fiddle that belonged to Grandma Paul—my mother's mother. I must have been in the fifth grade when I started lessons and played in the school orchestra through elementary and junior high. I probably should say I played at it. I never really cared enough about it to want to pursue it, and didn't really play it very well. Finally when I was a junior—I think—at La Jolla High there were so many things going on that I just couldn't practice, and I convinced my folks I was going to be a heckuva lot better golfer than I was a fiddler. So I quit.

I remember getting out of practicing the violin one time because of an accident. A bunch of us were carrying a great big rock that must have weighed a hundred pounds—it took three of us to move it—out to the end of the pier in front of our house. We wanted to throw it out into the bay and see how big a splash it would make.

We were about halfway out the pier when we just had to put it down to rest. Suddenly one of the guys—it might have been Willie Frazee, a friend I played with a lot in elementary school —told me I was bleeding. I looked down at my right hand and there was blood squirting out. It was really a mess. We had set the rock down on my finger but I never felt a thing. It didn't even hurt when I was looking at it.

It was a crisis around the house. It was a Sunday afternoon and Mom and Dad had a tough time finding a doctor to treat me. We finally went to the emergency hospital where they stitched me up. I couldn't straighten the finger out until a few years later. Playing touch football, just as I threw a pass, some guy blocked the ball and I broke the first knuckle on that finger. Now I can curl it around a golf club real well. The doctor who sewed me up was afraid I might lose part of that finger but I never did. All I have to show for it is a big scar and a bent knuckle.

If that hadn't turned out so fortunately, I might have ended up being a mechanic. My talents in that area really came in handy with one of the great events from my young years, getting a bike for Christmas—one with big balloon tires and those Longhorn handlebars. I was probably ten or eleven, and Jack and I along with other kids in the area used to go off on rides. The favorite was to pack a lunch and head down the ocean front to downtown San Diego. Then we'd pile on the old Coronado Island ferry, get off the boat and ride down by the Naval Air Station on the island to eat our lunch in a little bit of green we called the park. (Probably it was nothing more than a parkway alongside the road but in those days it seemed like a big park to us.)

That was quite a ride, taking the better part of the day. We had to leave early in the morning to be sure of getting a ferry back in time to be home before dark. I don't know exactly how far it was, but at least eight to ten miles each way—plenty demanding for a 10- or 11-year-old.

We didn't do it every week, but more like two or three times a year and usually in the summer when the days were long and warm. Once in a while we'd stop off on the way for a little swim if it was especially hot. The next day I'd go all over my bike. I did it often enough that I could take that coaster-brake bike apart in the dark, clean the sprocket, the gears and all the other running equipment with no problem. That may be where my interest in cars stems from. It also helped give me some importance with the other kids even though I was younger than most of them. They knew if something broke I always seemed able to patch it up or fix it so we could get home.

Those were beautiful years. Baseball, the bike, the surf, and the bay—all were big interests in my young life and the days never seemed long enough to hold everything. Soon they would be shorter yet. A new fascination was about to reach out and grab me.

6

ㅇ◼ㅇ◼ㅇ◼ㅇ◼ㅇ◼ㅇ◼ㅇ◼

It all started at the little Presidio Hills Pitch and Putt course in Old Town, a section of San Diego that's now a state park. It's only a block or two off the freeway leading up to hotel circle in the Mission Valley area and I was destined to know the route very well.

One day when I was about nine, according to Mom, she took all three of us—Dick, Jack and me—there to play with her. From that day on I was totally hooked. If I had my druthers any day I'd play golf.

I seemed to have a natural instinct for playing and my swing wasn't too bad. Mom used to call me the Ted Williams of golf—just kidding, of course. Ted grew up in San Diego as a great high school baseball player. By this time, however, he was in the major leagues with the Boston Red Sox and was one of my playground idols.

If my memory is good, Jack and I had to share a set of clubs. They were some old Gene Sarazen sticks on which Dad had cut the shafts down just a bit so they'd fit us. Dick, of course, was six years older and able to use regular length clubs.

My folks made golf very enjoyable for us kids. There was never any pressure to be good, score well or master the proper

38

swing. We just played for pleasure, and Presidio was a fun course. Weekends the whole family would play, and on weekdays we'd go up there in the morning with Mom and take our lunch along. After playing eighteen holes we'd sit on the grass and eat, and then usually play another round. You could get by with two clubs and a putter, and for fifty cents you could play all day.

Once I got bitten by the golf bug, I was always after Jack to play. He was two years older, and I needed someone to ride with me to Old Town. Clubs in hand, along with a brown bag lunch, we'd board the bus, ready to spend the whole day with Al Abrego, the owner of the Presidio course.

A great deal of the credit for my game has to go to Al Abrego. He used to give me a lot of little tips, especially when we'd go up alone to play. Al was a wonderful man and operated that golf course until he died in the spring of 1975.

The bus continued to get me around as golf became more important in my life, and I began to play in the junior tournaments. I can remember hauling my bag on bus after bus to get to Chula Vista, Balboa Park, and all the other courses in the San Diego area. Fortunately, golf bags weren't the huge hulks they are now. In fact, they weren't more than six inches across and with the woods and irons in them they were top-heavy. About the only way you could keep them from falling over as the buses rounded the corners or when you were carrying them on the course was by taking the two- and three-irons and sticking them upside down in the bag so there'd be some weight at the bottom.

I got a big kick out of a bus ride, and a bus ride to the golf course seemed to relax me. When I got to the course I was ready to play.

In the summer of 1940 my parents joined La Jolla Country Club. After that, there was no doubt what I wanted to be—a golf pro.

On the weekends we'd caddie for Mom and Dad and that was real fun. It took four hours or so to play around the course at La Jolla and you did a lot of walking. But I've always enjoyed that and still today much prefer walking to using a cart.

The first scrapbook I ever made dates from those days. The front page said, in big letters, GOLF. Under that I'd printed:

"MY DIARY OF GOLF, GENE LITTLER, BOOK ONE."

On the title page I had a little prayer.

> Lord, give me grace
> To make a score
> So low that even I,
> When talking of it afterwards,
> May never need to lie.

Some people have said that was a bit of original writing by me but I doubt it. I think I read or heard it somewhere although I have no idea where. It did leave a lasting impression, however. I can still quote that little saying whenever I am asked, even when several years elapse between requests.

One of the first things in that scrapbook was a little clipping from one of the papers recording my first hole in one on July 8, 1945, at Presidio. I made it on the fourteenth hole, a three-par 75-yard hole that I'd played a hundred times by then.

I used to have quite a few of those little certificates around. I scored another on March 29, 1949, on number ten at Presidio.

Even though my parents belonged to the La Jolla club we still played Presidio a lot because at certain times children weren't allowed on the country club course alone. Al Abrego never gave us any trouble even when we failed to replace our divots. He was just great with kids, so patient and so understanding.

One of the brightest memories of my young golf days, however, took place at La Jolla Country Club. I can still remember the date: January 25, 1942. I was eleven years old, in the sixth grade, and that day I played golf with my mom. It was the first time I ever broke 100 on a regulation golf course. I shot a 98 and received a certificate recording my score.

I also remember being overshadowed a bit by Mom; she scored a hole in one on the sixth hole. But the certificate I got that day still is a milestone in my memory. John Bellante, who signed it, was the first pro I knew at La Jolla, and he is one man who has to get a great deal of credit for whatever success I have had in golf.

After that I played a lot at La Jolla and from then on there was no way to keep me off the course. Jack and I would spend the morning scrounging for lost balls in the rough and the rest of the day playing golf. There was no water on La Jolla then but it had all kinds of rough—deep, deep rough—in the natural canyons and arroyos.

A lot of the older players who'd hit a ball into one of the arroyos made no effort to find the ball. You had to be half billy goat or all kid to get down to most of them. My dad used to tell me I was a bit of both with the number of balls I'd find.

I can't ever remember having to pay for a golf ball. When I was young I found all kinds of them, some as good as new. In the early months of World War II people didn't know or didn't believe there was going to be such a shortage of golf balls, but once that happened, there was a lot more searching for balls that went in the bushes, and you never threw any ball away. You'd play them with cuts, out of round, and pretty well beat-up. It seemed golf balls were harder to come by then than tires for cars. I can remember people having balls recovered and painted. Someone even produced a type of filler that could be used to fill a bad slash before they were repainted. Once they were repainted they weren't much good. The paint always peeled off, and it was nothing to hit a ball and knock a lot of paint off of it.

After I broke 100 my game just seemed to come on strong. I remember in 1943—before my thirteenth birthday in July— that I lowered my handicap at La Jolla ten strokes, going down to an eight. I was shooting consistently in the low 80s and once in a while breaking into the high 70s. That's not unusual for teenagers today but then it was a pretty good score for a kid.

In 1944, just after my fourteenth birthday, I won my first trophy in a special junior tournament for the La Jolla Country Club championship. Tom Meanley, a senior member and one of my greatest boosters as a young golfer, put up a $25 War Bond for the winner. Ironically, it was his son, Bobby, that I beat with my 75. Bobby shot a 77.

Early that same summer, on the first day of June to be exact, when I was still thirteen, I went around the La Jolla course under par for the first time. I shot a 35–35—70, which was then two under par. That was one of the most exciting days of my life. I'd dreamed about breaking par for so long and had come close before but never quite made it.

All I did nearly every daylight hour that summer was play golf, along with two or three other juniors. We usually went off early in the morning and late in the day so we wouldn't interfere with the regular members.

I remember going down to the club one day on my motor scooter. Bobby Meanley, one of the juniors who played every day, was driving, and I was sitting on the back unwrapping a piece of candy. Bobby ran over the streetcar tracks, making the scooter zigzag suddenly, and off I went. I slid about fifty feet into the curb and was very lucky there weren't any cars coming from the other direction.

I was skinned from top to bottom, but we went on to the club and played golf. When I got home that night Mom was ready to take me apart. She had been talking to someone up at the club who had seen me come in all scratched and bloody. Mom was already worried when I traded off my bike to get that scooter, but after this incident she never really had much peace until I got rid of it.

In the summer of 1944 I probably made more progress as a golfer than during any other period in my life. I always played thirty-six holes at La Jolla and sometimes, if I could find transportation, I'd get in another eighteen or thirty-six at Presidio working on my short game. The only limiting factor was daylight. Many a round I played more by feel than by sight.

By then the war was on full bore and San Diego was solid with sailors, Marines, Coast Guard, and Army personnel. We lived under blackout regulations, which meant I had to be home before dark or walk since car lights were restricted.

Still, golf was most of my life. When school started in the

fall I could hardly wait for classes to be out so I could get up to the country club and play.

During Christmas vacation of that year—December 21 to be exact—I played the best round of my life until then. I shot a 67—five under par—and realized a longstanding goal of breaking 70.

Shortly after shooting that 67 I received an invitation to participate in the Los Angeles Open—I was fourteen and they told me I was the youngest player they had ever invited—but I had to pass it up. Gas rationing was on at the time and we couldn't drive up to Los Angeles.

7

Christmas of 1944 was celebrated for several days, thanks to that 67. But, more important, I played golf from sunrise to sunset. I was totally hooked. All those folks who belonged to La Jolla Country Club then must have thought I was part of the equipment. I was always there. Mom knew by then there was no use planning dinner for me before it got dark. And even then I'd have to get home, usually late.

I was still in junior high and trying to squeeze in time for the violin in the orchestra, a little basketball and baseball, and throwing the shot on the track team. One thing for sure: there wasn't any time to get into any trouble. It seemed like I was forever due someplace.

My wife claims that living on that kind of timetable when I was growing up is what has made me such a punctual person as an adult. Nothing irritates me more than having an appointment for which the other person is late. I know, of course, that you can get caught in traffic or have a car break down or something. But I have to say I really appreciate time and its value.

I was very fortunate to have been born and raised in San Diego. Not only is the climate conducive to golf—I can hardly remember any two days in my life when I couldn't play—but our junior program gave us a lot of valuable experience. Those of us who grew up in San Diego—fellows like Phil Rodgers, Frank Morey, Billy Casper, Bobby Gardner and all the others —played in so many tournaments in junior high, high school, college, and amateur events that we had a tremendous advantage when the big ones rolled around. The pressure just wasn't as much for us as for someone who had played in only a few tournaments.

The ability to make mental preparation for tournament play in golf is something you can only acquire by playing. Playing friends or at the club just doesn't give you the edge you need mentally. That has to come with playing *for* something, and a tournament with a title keeps you getting sharp each day. You know you'll be facing competitors who could break par in any given round. So you work like the devil so you can break par every time you go out.

My first real competitive show was in the summer of 1945 in the San Diego County Junior championships. The tournament was played at the San Diego Country Club, and I finished second to my buddy, Frank Morey, Jr. Frank was the son of a naval officer and quite a hero among the kids. He'd been living in Honolulu when the Japanese attacked Pearl Harbor December 7, 1941, and was finally sent back to the mainland with his mother. To the kids he was like a Marine or Navy veteran— he'd been in combat.

That day in '45 when Frank won, I shot pretty consistent golf, considering the fact that it was the most prestigious tournament I had ever been in. My rounds were 75-75-74-78 for a 302 total. While that score didn't bring me a title, it was pretty good for someone who had just turned fifteen at the beginning of the summer season. Frank beat me quite easily— by seven strokes—with rounds of 74-74-74-73 and 295.

I was in high school in 1945 and La Jolla High, for the first time, had a golf team. We even had a class in physical education that included golf etiquette. Our golf coach—Larry Hanson—would take us over to La Jolla Country Club and John Bellante, the pro, would instruct us on proper consideration on the course. One of the members of the golf team that year was

Art Barnard, who went on to be a champion high hurdler at the University of Southern California. My brother Jack was also on the team one year.

As the years passed and I became more mature and more confident in tournament play, I began to win more events. A great many of them were played against friends who grew up with me in San Diego. Many of them, like Frank Morey, who is the professional at Wilshire Country Club in Los Angeles, are still my close friends today.

I took a fling at basketball and track at La Jolla High School. I wasn't big enough for football. (Probably the real reason was that I didn't want to give the time to it, and being too small was just another factor.) I played basketball one year and was on the track team running a little and putting the shot.

In spite of my size I was pretty strong. For quite a while I held the Class B shot-put record at about 52′ 10″ or so. But when I became too old for the B-team and had to move up to the varsity and the 12-pound shot, I had to work a little harder to be competitive.

But basketball and track still didn't compare to golf. If I had a choice, I was always at the country club.

In the early summer of 1946 I played in the San Diego County Amateur Championships and won the first flight. That's the first bracket below the championship, which was won by Harry LeBarron, Jr.

In July of that year I finally beat Frank Morey for the County Junior title but I had a little advantage since it was played at La Jolla Country Club. I could almost play that course in the dark or blindfolded. I had two sensational rounds 75–69–69–78 for 291 and Frank shot 73–76–74–75 for 298.

During those years in San Diego we also played in the Harvey Fleming Scholarship Tournament. This was an event for juniors, and the winner received a $200 scholarship. The three scholarships I won in 1946, 1947, and 1948 ultimately came in handy when I enrolled at San Diego State. I never really knew who Harvey Fleming was, but we always got the award from a vice-president of the First National Bank.

That fall, in September, 1946, I played in my first open tournament, finishing fourth in the San Diego County Open, tied with Merle Lint. Bobby Gardner, who was then going to UCLA, won the title with 288 and I scored 295. Although it was played at La Jolla Country Club, my rounds were not impressive, but sure consistent—74–74–73–74.

In the voting for San Diego "golfer of the year" in 1946 I was second to Gardner, which was flattering, since Bobby was in his mid-twenties and I was just past sixteen.

That November I won the La Jolla men's club championship for the first time. My 74–72–74–73 for 293 beat Loren Jacks, who had a 297. The La Jolla Country Club Newsletter for December 1, 1946, carried this paragraph: "Let's take our hats off to the new club champion, Gene Littler, who won the tournament with a comfortable lead. Gene is not only a fine young man but an excellent golfer with a wonderful future."

All my success in golf was nice, but if you had asked me in 1946 what the most important event was I'd have told you my sixteenth birthday. That was on July 21. And it was important for one big reason. That's when I could get a driver's license under California law.

I'd been worrying my folks crazy with that Cushman motor scooter. Ever since I'd sailed off it when Bobby Meanley hit the streetcar tracks, Mom was always afraid I was going to end up dead in one of the gullies going to and from the country club.

So after I had passed the driver's test and had my license, I never quit talking about getting my own car. I'd tinkered around with the folks' Buick all the time. I was hooked on cars almost the way I was on golf. There were some who wondered if golf wasn't second, even though in my mind it was definitely first.

I had learned to drive when I was fourteen or fifteen, and I'd been saving my money for a long time so that I'd be able to buy one just as soon as I could get a license. You could tell how serious I was by the number of hours I worked every summer around the country club doing odd jobs and caddying. I was up before dawn and over there to sweep dew off the greens with those big old long bamboo poles. There were several of us who'd shag balls on the driving range, caddy when we could and do anything else they wanted.

But that job and my intense desire to drive nearly had the wrong ending. Jack and I were sweeping the greens one morning when we noticed the old Model A pick-up truck the greens-keeper used to make the rounds. The key was in the ignition and we couldn't resist the temptation to use it. I was doing pretty good with it until I slipped into a huge hole alongside one of the fairways and got stuck. We tried everything we could think of to get that Model A out of that wallow but nothing worked.

It seemed like a long time until the greenskeeper came to work and we could go up and tell him what had happened. I don't recall any longer how they got it out, but it was really mired down in that hole. It's a wonder we weren't fired but I'm sure we were warned never to take the truck again.

My dad gave us the devil—I guess not so much for taking it but for the chance of getting hurt if we had rolled it over or the damage we could have done if it had got away from us and torn up the course.

Even that incident couldn't stop me with cars. From the time I was big enough to crawl up behind the wheel of our big old Buick, I put on a lot of mileage, never leaving the drive nor ever having the engine on. So you can imagine how I was after that sixteenth birthday came by.

8

The day my dad came home and told me he thought he knew where he could get me a car if I wanted it I about went through the roof. I never did figure out why there was an "if" about it.

It didn't matter to me that it was nearly as old as I was. My mother's father—Alexander Paul—had owned it originally, but it now belonged to the Hazard Company, and they were willing to part with it. It was a 1933 two-door Ford—thirteen years old and a little beyond the usable age for a construction company. Anyway, Hazard told Dad I could have it for $150. What a buy. I could hardly wait to get the $150 out of the bank and pick up that car.

Dad went with me to the Hazard yard, which was over in Mission Valley not too far from the stadium where the San Diego Padres and the Chargers play. It still ran pretty good for a '33. It had a V-8 engine of about 85 horsepower, a stick shift, of course, and from then on if I wasn't playing golf or in school I was out in the yard working on that Ford.

I never took auto shop in high school or had much help fixing cars but I went to work on that car as if it was some jewel.

49

I bought a little spray outfit and some body hammers to iron out the creases and dents.

I was completely fascinated. Mom or Dad had to come out every night and literally grab me by the neck to come in and go to bed. I didn't try to do much to the engine—I didn't know how—but I checked books out of the library and learned how to do body work, prime-paint the body, and do light tune-up and adjustments.

For weeks I mulled over what color I was going to paint it. Finally, after looking at about every color swatch at the paint store, I settled on a medium green. I can't tell you if it was lacquer or just plain old paint. All I know is that '33 Ford got the most tender loving care any kid could lavish on a car.

It was a super car. Ran like a top. Every kid in school must have chipped in with advice on what to do to the inside and the outside of the Green Hornet, as I called it, but I just let them talk. I already had my own ideas.

That car did a lot more than just create conversation among the gang. It gave me an interest in life that still haunts me today and it gave me wheels to get around to play in more golf tournaments and get in more practice.

If you really pinned me down right now as to what I prefer —playing golf or fixing up cars—I'd have to give the answer a lot of thought. I sure do love this game of golf, but when I've been out on tour two or three weeks I find myself every evening looking over my calendar to see exactly the date I return to San Diego to see my family and my cars.

With World War II over, many of the things that were rationed, such as gasoline and tires, were available and it was pretty tough for my folks to keep track of me. It wasn't that I was doing anything terrible, but it was nothing for me to play thirty-six holes a day, forty-five on some days, and, if the weather was right, toss in a fifty-four-hole day.

I remember driving to La Mesa in January (a city east of San Diego a few miles) to play in the San Diego County Junior Championships. I beat Gene Woemper 2 and 1 in match play, shooting a 68. That win seemed to give me a lot of confidence and I continued to play well, taking top honors in another Harvey Fleming Fund Tournament in July. Earlier that month at the San Diego County Fairgrounds they held a driving contest. It was not only for distance but for accuracy and I scored 35 points to win that part of it. I nearly had the longest drive too at 299 yards, but a pro named Hector Clark hit one out 299 yards and 2 inches to beat me.

There was no doubt now that my game was coming on fast. Every tournament I learned more about championship competition, especially to control my own emotions and not let mistakes bother me.

In July of 1947 my buddy, Frank Morey, and I qualified to play in the National Junior Chamber of Commerce championships. The tournament was being held at the Mount Hawley Country Club in Peoria, Illinois, and I'll never forget that trip.

We went by train, and in those days, with the public finally getting able to move around following the war, it was rough to get accommodations. So we had to ride a chair car. It didn't even have upholstered seats, just those old hard wicker jobs with little ventilation holes in them. No air-conditioning, of course. That was the hottest train I ever recall being on, and it took almost three days with a change or two to reach Peoria, a place I'd never heard of.

We qualified well and were fortunate to draw into opposite brackets. Our goal was to make it an all-San Diego final since it was at match play. We were sponsored by the San Diego Junior Chamber and Frank was playing real good golf, having beat me in three straight tournaments before heading east.

We got to the semifinals but here our plan fell apart. Frank lost 1-up to Al Mengert, who later became a very fine touring professional, but I made the finals with a 4 and 3 victory over George Dial from Columbia, South Carolina.

It was disappointing not to have the chance to play Frank, because the Junior Chamber people in San Diego had been so good to us. But since Frank was out of the finals he caddied for me. It wasn't my day either. I'd got some kind of a bug the night before and was up all night. It probably wouldn't have made any difference. Mengert was the defending champion and gave me a pretty good lesson in winning.

My putting was bad. They just wouldn't drop. And, I suppose, between being sick and losing the psychological desire with Frank's defeat, it wouldn't have made too much difference.

The next year, however, I won the National Junior Chamber title in Lincoln, Nebraska, beating Dick Yost in the semifinals and scoring a 3 and 2 win over Morris Williams of Texas in the finals. Altogether I played in the Jaycees championship three times, losing in 1949 to Bud Holscher, 6 and 5.

The trip back from Peoria that first time in 1947 was one to remember. This time we were fortunate. We got a berth to sleep in—one berth. The only way Frank and I could figure out to make it work was to sleep at opposite ends. Only trouble was that every time one of us turned over we poked the other in the face with our feet.

It's a funny kind of memory to cherish. But we were young then, and it was our first experience—at least it was mine—on a train.

Later that summer, in the California Golf Association Medal Play Championship at Mission Valley Country Club, I played one of my best competitive tournaments to that time. Most of the top amateurs in the state were entered, and I beat Bobby Gardner by a stroke, my first big win as a youngster. For the four rounds I shot 283; Gardner had 284; and Johnny Dawson, one of the all-time greats of amateur golf who later gave me one of my biggest steps upwards, had 285. Besides Gardner and Dawson there were some other standouts in the field like Bob Rosburg and Bruce McCormick, one of the perennial amateur champions in the state.

Back in those days it seems there was an amateur golf tournament of some importance almost every week. One of the funniest incidents—although at the time I didn't think it was too funny—happened in the summer of 1948 after I had come back from Lincoln where I had won the Jaycee title.

The National Amateur championship was scheduled for Pebble Beach. In order to play we had to qualify. They were

holding the qualifying rounds in Los Angeles on two courses—
Riviera and Bel Air. Frank Morey and I drove up in that little
'33 Ford that was my pride and joy and got a motel somewhere in the Santa Monica area. After a practice round one
day we were driving around trying to decide where to eat.

I'm not real sure, but I think Frank was driving when the
transmission dropped in the little Green Bomb and all we
ended up able to use was second gear. Now we had a problem. We had drawn different courses on which to qualify. Since
it was a one-day, 36-hole qualifying we had some figuring to
do.

Frank drove me to Bel Air and dropped me off that morning
because I was going off the tee much earlier. Then he drove to
Riviera for his first round. I hitched a ride to Riviera for my
second round and Frank crept over to Bel Air in second gear
for his second eighteen.

I don't know if the car had anything to do with it or not, but
we didn't qualify. I do remember that it took us forever to drive
home to San Diego in second gear. We couldn't go over thirty
miles per hour. We drove the Pacific Coast Highway all the
way home (in those days there was no San Diego Freeway)
and everyone who passed us—and that was everyone on the
road—would look around and wonder what those two kids
were doing driving so slow in that lowered V-8.

In the middle of September—September 16, 1948, to be exact—I was honored by the San Diego Chamber of Commerce
for outstanding service in amateur athletics. I think it was the
first time I'd ever been given an award by my native city, and
my dad kind of needled me about it because I was having
some problems at the time concerning my car. I had sold my
little '33 and bought a '36 Ford coupe. It was quite a machine
and I had learned a great deal about fixing cars up with my
first Ford. But I was also spending a lot of my Saturday morn-
ings down at the Juvenile Traffic Court trying to explain why
my Smitty mufflers weren't off the car. They were quite loud,
and somewhere along the line I had learned you could get a
deeper "brrruuum-brrruum" if you plugged the heat risers in

the manifold with pennies that had a small hole drilled in them
—they fit perfectly. We'd heat the springs white hot so they'd
bend lowering the riding level of the car in the back. Then we
had to drive with care over every bump so we wouldn't rip out
the rear end. I don't think we were any menace to society but
we were loud.

9

One of my great memories of high school was a summertime exhibition Frank Morey and I played at La Jolla Country Club as a fund-raising effort for the Breitbard Athletic Foundation in San Diego. That was a facility created by Bob Breitbard, the man who built the San Diego Sports Arena and who founded the San Diego Rockets and the San Diego Gulls hockey club, now called the Mariners.

We played with Bobby Locke, the famed South African golfer who always wore knickers, and Lew Worsham, who was the National Open champion at the time. It was a 36-hole exhibition and we attracted quite a crowd for something like that.

Locke was the leading money winner of the tour at the time and along with Worsham was considered one of the top five pros in the world. The match took place on June 8, 1948, and they charged $1.50 per person to be in the gallery.

Worsham and I were paired together against Locke and Frank. Locke, one of the classic men of golf, not only wore knickers all the time but a shirt with a tie. I don't think there was another pro around at the time that wore a necktie. I really didn't see—and I still don't—how with a tie Bobby got enough freedom to really swing the club.

The talk around the course from men who knew of Locke and his ability indicated that quite a number of people in the golf world had tried to make a lot of money betting against Locke in head-to-head matches and he broke every one of them.

All I know for fact is that on this particular afternoon Bobby Locke was a picture of perfection and elegance. He never got a hair out of place nor ruffled his knickers as he put together rounds of 68–68—136. Worsham wasn't too shabby either. He shot 68–70—138. And I was a pretty happy kid since I shot the best round of all with a 67 in the afternoon to go with my 75 in the morning for a 142. Frank was Mr. Consistent with back to back 74s for a 148.

Worsham and I won the match, 2-up, but the score was incidental to the pleasure and enjoyment of two young high schoolers being paired with two of golf's great stars of the day.

I still have clippings in my scrapbooks from that match. Bobby Locke was extremely kind to us. "Those boys really shook us up," he told the press. "Give those boys a few years and they'll be getting the headlines on the golf circuit. They are among the most promising young fellows I have ever seen."

Well, you can imagine how Gene Littler and Frank Morey felt when those remarks appeared in the *San Diego Union* and *Tribune*. We were pretty hard to live with. A lot of our friends gave us a bad time, insisting we had put Locke up to making the remarks.

That was impossible. We were too nervous to do much more than call him Mr. Locke and even his partner Mr. Worsham.

I had a little advantage on Frank since we were playing on my home course. I held the course record there of 66 and earlier in the summer had beat Frank's course mark at San Diego Country Club, where he was a member, with a 65. But I've always felt that the round I shot that afternoon in company with Locke and Worsham was one of the better ones I played as a youngster. We were out there with two of the best and a large gallery of people who knew us. To shoot a 67 then was quite a feat.

With high school behind me—I graduated a few days after

the exhibition with Locke and Worsham—the question was, what next?

In those days it was tough even to think about going right into pro golf. There weren't the big dollars around and you could be certain there were no sponsors willing to back anyone on tour.

San Diego State, which was a state college then rather than a university as it now is, had a good athletic program and offered a few of us golf scholarships. They really weren't worth too much since we would live at home and tuition then was peanuts compared to what it costs to attend college today.

So in September of 1948 I enrolled at State and joined Frank Morey who was a year ahead of me. We had the makings of a pretty fair country golf team because we also had Lloyd Schunemann and Joe Weikel who were going to college up on the hill. Bud Holscher, who beat me in the Junior Chamber finals one year, decided to come to San Diego State too. He lived with me at our home but lasted only a semester or so of school before he quit.

Bud and I probably had the same theory on college: no particular goals or objectives in mind—just golf and more golf. School didn't mean much to me at the time (looking back on it, that was probably a mistake) but golf was my passion. I was a general business major but Dad always said that my minor dominated—recreation. That was his way of saying golf. I arranged my classes so I could be on the Mission Valley course (now the Stardust Hotel course) by noon every day. I'd get in eighteen holes plus some practice, and if the weather was good and the days were long, it would be twenty-seven and in some cases thirty-six.

My parents had separated and finally divorced during my final year of high school. It was pretty traumatic for us all. I lived with Mom in our house on La Mancha, and Bud Holscher stayed there also for that semester or so he attended San Diego State.

There weren't many classes that stood between any of us and a golf tournament. One we never missed was held every Easter vacation in Palm Springs—the O'Donnell Invitational Tournament, a prestige amateur event in Southern California. Going there in 1949 turned out to be a great misfortune.

Frank Morey and I drove down in my '36 Ford coupe. I had hundreds of hours invested in that car, leading out the body, pounding out all the dings, and painting it to where it shone like a mirror. It was lowered, and I had upholstered it to where it was one of the fine cars around for its day.

I don't recall just what route we took because the roads have changed so drastically over the years, but we went up the old Pacific Coast Highway and cut inland to go through Hemet, planning to come in by the back door to Palm Springs. We left about 9:30 in the morning, and as we moved inland it became hotter and hotter although this was late March or early April.

All of a sudden, as we were trying to get over the mountains, the Ford began to boil. We had no choice but to stop and let her cool off. To pass the time Frank and I climbed up on the front fenders and began to play gin rummy.

We were due in Palm Springs around noon so we could play a practice round with a fellow I had met named Bob Littler— no relation. He was a prominent clothier in Seattle and wanted me to join him in his business in Washington. But we never made more than one hill at a time, it seemed, so along about noon we found a phone at one of our many pit stops and called to tell him we wouldn't make it. I thought I was a pretty good mechanic—and I was, on the outside of a car—but I couldn't figure out what our problem was. And on this particular highway there weren't many places to repair a car or even get water.

Finally, about 5:30 P.M., we made Palm Springs, too late for golf but not too late to discover that a slipping fan belt was our problem. Morey never let me forget the calamity caused by a minor malfunction. He continually chided me about being a mechanic. But that I am not. Not even today.

That evening, as Morey was taking me regularly in gin and cribbage, we suddenly heard a big crash. We went outside our motel room to investigate. Some drunk had smashed into my Ford. He was so loaded he had a tough time giving his name and address, but I was so mad for what he had done to my little jewel that I wasn't too coherent myself.

Going back into the motel, we passed under a tree, and I just reached up and grabbed a limb about two inches in diameter and gave it a yank. I didn't realize it was covered with thorns until it broke and came down on my head. It raked my face all over, and, in fact, one of the thorns embedded itself in my scalp. Frank had to pull it out and put a bandage on to stop the bleeding.

You can imagine how I looked the next day at tee-off time in the O'Donnell Classic. I don't think anyone believed my story, even with Frank to corroborate it, so finally I just gave up and shrugged off the questions.

In the final weeks of my first year at San Diego State, we were entered in the National Collegiate Athletic Association championships to be played at the University of New Mexico. The other two members of our team, Lloyd Schunemann, who also ran the quarter and half mile for State, and Joe Weikel, had gone ahead to Albuquerque.

Frank and I had to wait because we were playing in the finals of San Diego County Amateur. We played the finals in the morning and I won, 8 and 7. After that we piled into a 1948 Chrysler that belonged to my stepfather, Dr. Robert Lowry, and took off for Albuquerque. We were going along at a pretty good clip through those flatlands when we had a blowout on the back left tire. The car started to waddle all over the highway but I just grabbed the wheel and held on as we slowed down. There wasn't much left but shreds of rubber when we pulled off on the shoulder. We changed the tire and went on into Albuquerque where we picked up a spare. But the tempo was set that didn't spell success.

It was blazing hot. Our rooms weren't air-conditioned. Frank and I qualified for match play but Lloyd and Joe didn't. Frank lost in the first round and I was eliminated in the second. We couldn't wait to get out of New Mexico (where, by the way, Frank's son is now a member of the golf team and playing to a one handicap).

We took off from the golf course and headed the Chrysler west. We didn't stop until we pulled into the driveway on La Mancha.

I'm always glad to get home. But I was really happy to be back this time—mainly because of an acquaintance I had made just before the close of the fall term at State at the Blue Book Ball.

10

No one ever called me a social lion. There just didn't seem to be enough time for much of that side of college life. There was one young lady on campus, however, who had caught my eye many, many times . . . especially in a large history lecture class where I sat a row or two behind her.

It was one of those classes where you're just a number in a class of three hundred or so. I had mentioned to Frank that this was sure an attractive girl. He kept telling me to call her for a date but I never did. Maybe I was bashful—I really don't know—but it was tough for me to call a girl and ask her out.

Each year State celebrated the completion of finals with the Blue Book Ball. It was named after the blue books we used for final exams and it was a huge dance to celebrate the close of the academic year.

Frank was going with a girl named Dorothy Logan, who later became his wife and the mother of his four children. Dorothy knew the girl in my history class. So did another fellow in our fraternity, Omega Xi—Bill Cowling, who was going to the dance with this girl's best friend, Marilyn Taliaferro. One night Frank just dialed the phone and handed it to me. It was like staring down at a putt. You have to swing the club, and I had to talk.

That's how I met Shirley Mae Warren. She said she'd go to the Blue Book Ball with me, and we've been going places together ever since.

Cowling and Morey gave me nothing but trouble after I had hung up because I wasn't so sure I should go to a dance. I wasn't much on dancing. In fact, I was pretty awful, but I was attracted enough to Shirley to hustle up in my best dark suit when it was time for the ball. It was quite an affair as dances go. As I recall, it was held at a large ballroom in Mission Beach. The girls wore long party dresses. There might have been a tux or two among the guys who had them or the money to rent one but I'd say most just wore dark suits.

We had little tiny Blue Books where the girls kept track of the dances. I was out on the floor a lot but I felt sorry for Shirley. She'd never met me before and I had to be the worst dancer on the whole floor.

That blind date—and I guess it wasn't really blind because I had seen Shirley a lot and just hadn't had the courage to ask her out—started something that's never ended. It wasn't one of those meetings that turned into a whirlwind courtship leading to the altar forty-eight hours later. I kept asking Shirley out and she kept going out with me, and neither one of us can really pin down a date when we decided to marry. I just assumed we would and we did.

We discovered we had lived relatively close together for many years. Shirley had attended Point Loma High while I was at La Jolla but until we saw one another at San Diego State we were not aware of each other.

Shirley's parents were both schoolteachers. Her dad taught history and music and later on headed the psychological testing department for the San Diego school system. Both her parents played the piano well and her father, who was a graduate of the American Conservatory of Music in Chicago, used to play professionally in dance bands during the depression.

It was difficult for Shirley to understand all the demands

golf put on my time. When other guys were hanging around campus drinking Cokes and talking, I was out at the golf course practicing. If not, then I was playing a tournament somewhere.

I remember coming home one time from the Tucson Invitational Best Ball Championship with Morey. We had won some fine looking watches but Shirley couldn't see what the big deal was about a watch and a golf tournament.

She did understand the day I had one of the best rounds of golf I ever shot at La Jolla Country Club. That was in the early spring of 1950. There were five of us playing, including J. W. Bostick, Joe Beardsley, Hector Clark, and John Bellante, the club pro. It was one of the hottest rounds of golf I ever shot in my life.

At that time the course was 36–36—par 72. Over the years they have revised various holes, but it was fairly long and tight. I shot the front nine in 31. Everything I hit was right on and I have seldom putted better. I came home in 32 for a 63.

That broke the course record of 64 I had set on December 31, 1949, when I had seven birdies in a row. But my round of 63 was nine under par and, while it didn't include a string like that of the year before, it was a fine round.

Before I picked up Shirley that night her dad had told her about my round. Since he had taken up golf about this time, he was impressed with the score. So was I. So was Shirley. From then on she began to pay more and more attention to golf and today she's mighty sharp on the game although she doesn't really play.

My social life improved tremendously after the Blue Book Ball. There weren't too many affairs at State we didn't attend. A great many of them we went to with Frank and Dorothy or Bill and Marilyn.

Omega Xi fraternity (later on a chapter of Kappa Alpha, a national) was pretty much made up of athletes at State. Frank and I were golfers. Joe Alston was the National Badminton champion and a fellow named Alex Gordon was later the tennis pro at the Hotel Del Coronado. We all felt we were pretty good all-around athletes. We figured out this round robin sports competition whereby the one with the most talent would give the others a handicap in his own specialty. For example, I played their best ball in golf. Gordon would play us tennis using the singles court and we would use the doubles. It was similar in badminton. But in the end each guy won in his sport so we never really proved a thing. But we had a lot of fun.

During my two years at San Diego State, I played in what I still consider one of the most memorable golf matches of my life. It came in the California State Amateur at Pebble Beach in October 1949 with MacGregor Hunter, whose father, Willie Hunter, was then head professional at Riviera Country Club.

I was five down after the morning eighteen. I had not played well on one of the great golf courses of the world. But in the afternoon things began to fall into place. By the 35th hole I had evened the match after chipping into the hole over Mac's ball, which had me stymied.

We were both on the final green in three—15 to 18 feet from the cup. I was away with a sidehill putt and I made it, the ball breaking nearly two feet to drop in. I was a pretty happy kid when it dropped. Lloyd Schuneman, who had come up to caddy for me, was jubilant, yelling and pounding me on the back, and the gallery joined in.

That appeared to be the match as Mac had a tough 15-footer to tie me. But he rammed that putt home as if the ball had eyes and we had to go extra holes, sudden death.

We went to the 37th hole—the first tee—and both had good drives. Mac was away and his second shot, while not a bad one, bounced down into the deep trap on the right side of the green. With the pin placed on the far right, his next shot was a difficult one. I was pretty sure he couldn't make a par from that lie. I played it safe and shot to the left side of the green where I would have a good chance for my par. I was confident I couldn't lose the hole and figured if I could get down in two the California State Amateur was mine for the first time.

Mac climbed down carefully into the bunker. After considerable time weighing the club and making several adjustments with his grip, he swung. It was a beautiful shot out of the sand. As I watched its flight and saw it trickle into the cup, I was dumbfounded. My ball was off the putting surface about two feet and I decided to try a chip. Another right move, as I holed the shot.

On to 38. Here we halved the hole with birdies. We were still tied going to 39, and some wondered how long this could go on. So did I. It ended a few minutes later when I took three to get down from off the green to the left and MacGregor took two to end one of the most exciting matches I ever played. You had to be there to appreciate the full impact.

Some years later Verne Wickham, a longtime golf writer in Southern California, wrote a piece about that match. He bracketed it with other famous matches at Pebble Beach: the time in 1929 when Johnny Goodman beat the fabled Bobby Jones for the National Amateur . . . the day in 1947 Johnny Dawson lost a historic battle to Skee Riegel in another National Amateur final on that historic course hard by the Pacific Ocean . . . and some of the many fine final rounds in Bing Crosby's big clambake that is such a major factor on the winter tour.

"None of these," Wickham wrote, "have been the thriller Littler and Hunter played that day back in 1949." It was truly a phenomenal match because so many exciting things happened toward the end and in the extra holes. I really don't know who was disappointed most, me or Lloyd, who had agonized over every shot all through that 39 hole final.

Near the end of my second year at San Diego State, Shirley and I had pretty well decided that we were for each other and to get married. I was not what you would call a student. My grades were adequate but no one ever recommended me for Phi Beta Kappa or any fellowship unless golf was the course major.

My namesake, Bob Littler, had been after me for months to move up to Seattle and join his men's clothing business. After finals in June of 1950 I decided to give it a whirl. I thought it might be a good opportunity to learn a good business. I wasn't sure about professional golf yet. But deep down I really wanted to take a shot at it some day.

Just about the time I arrived in Seattle to start at the bottom working in the stock room, the Korean War broke out. A few days before the Fourth of July I remember listening to President Truman ordering General Douglas MacArthur, the Army and the Navy to join in the defense of South Korea.

That made me a little anxious because my older brother, Dick, was in service. I was up in Seattle alone and finding no personal enjoyment whatsoever about any facet of the clothing business. I did find enough time to play quite a bit, but I sure didn't want to try to make a living in the retail clothing business.

That stay in Seattle made me understand just how important Shirley was in my life. She had gotten a summer job at Grand Canyon working as a waitress at the El Tovar Hotel. On my way home from the NCAA I stopped by Grand Canyon to see her. And a few weeks later before going home to get ready to return to San Diego State she came up to Seattle to visit.

She decided to stay in Seattle to see if I was going to hack it as a clothing salesman. She went to work in a furniture company for a man named Lynch, whom I had met at a tournament at the Broadmoor Country Club in Seattle.

As summer moved into fall, the rains became more and more regular in Seattle. Not only was it wet and cold but it was pretty hard to play much golf in those conditions. By the first part of October I'd had it in Seattle. I felt bad about pulling out on Bob Littler, but he had recognized long before I did that the men's clothing business wasn't for me.

It was a pretty trying time all the way around. Shirley's parents were being divorced, the war was on, and a lot of guys I knew were being drafted and sent over to Korea. We got back to San Diego about the first week in October, too late for either of us to return to State. It wasn't long until we had become engaged and I had decided to enlist in the Navy.

Shortly before Christmas the Navy notified me that I would be called the early part of January. Almost overnight Shirley and I decided to be married before I went into boot camp, because once they skinned off my hair we wouldn't see civilization for a month.

You can imagine, with Christmas coming up, what a scramble we had getting everything lined up for the wedding and trying to find a place to live. I don't think I took a club out of my bag for nearly a month. Somehow, some way—mainly thanks to Shirley's thorough organizational ability—things fell into place with our wedding day right on top of us.

11 ○■○■○■○■○■○■○■○

On the morning of January 5, 1951, a lot of my golfing buddies were just starting the first round in the annual Los Angeles Open being played at Riviera Country Club. But golf was the least thing on my mind. Whatever had to be done to get ready for our wedding was done, and only the ceremony remained. It worried me a lot more to think about a little walk of seventy-five feet or so down the aisle than if I'd been staring down at a putt of that distance at Riviera in the Open.

I've always been an early riser but I was up a lot before the sun that morning. I was still living at home up on La Mancha Drive. Jack, my middle brother, was my best man so I had someone to commiserate with as we got ready for the ceremony.

Now don't get me wrong. There was nothing in the world more important then and now than Shirley. I couldn't wait to have her become my wife, but I was never one for pomp and ceremony. But you only get married once and I was steeled to do the best I could. It was like dancing. I was a poor dancer and I was afraid I wouldn't be as good a bridegroom as Shirley should have. But I was mighty happy and proud to be there just the same.

Shirley was just a dream. I'll never forget looking down that aisle when they played the wedding march and she came toward me on her father's arm. She wore a long soft white satin dress that was quite special with lots of lace. I'd known for a long, long time that Gene Littler was the luckiest man alive to be marrying Shirley Mae Warren. But when she came down the aisle she was just beautiful.

We were married in the La Jolla Presbyterian Church which is still at 7715 Draper Street downtown. The Reverend George G. Culbertson performed the ceremony. I did pretty well with all the I do's but if I'd been a quarterback they'd have called me for backfield in motion when I slipped one of the double gold wedding bands on Shirley's finger. I finally made it, but if I'd been trying to hole out a two-foot putt the ball would still be rolling.

Shirley tells me we didn't have a formal wedding. I guess that's right because I doubt if you could ever get me into a set of tails or a frock coat. I had a rough enough time with a tux and cravat collar.

The wedding was really simple. It was a family affair and not too large. It's hard to remember numbers now but as I recall we sent out somewhere between a hundred and a hundred and fifty invitations, and most of those invited came.

One of the nice things about it was that most of those in the wedding party were all old, old friends. Grace Bentley, who played the wedding march on the organ, was a sorority sister of Shirley's at San Diego State. Joan Sieger, the vocalist, was in the same sorority.

Shirley's maid of honor was Marilyn Taliaferro, her best friend, who along with Bill Cowling had really set up the blind date we had at the Blue Book Ball. Marilyn is now Mrs. David Hall and lives in Phoenix.

The reception, a quiet, friendly affair, was held at the La Jolla Country Club, the place that has been close and dear to me over all these wonderful years.

We didn't have much time for a honeymoon. January 5th was a Friday and Shirley had to be back at work at Convair Monday morning. I don't know exactly when we left La Jolla but it was late afternoon. We had reservations at the Normandy Village Inn in Palm Springs, now the Normandy Hotel, at the same location.

We drove down to Palm Springs in the third car I ever owned, a 1941 Ford, which ran a good deal better than the earlier one Frank Morey and I had so much trouble with. This one was a coupe and I had practically rebuilt it. It was painted a navy blue and had a medium blue pleated upholstery. As I recall I had the upholstery work done in San Diego and I thought it was the most beautiful job ever.

Our honeymoon was over almost before it began since we had to leave Sunday so Shirley could get to work and I had a lot of things to do for the Navy.

Thanks to Shirley's dad we had found a very small furnished apartment on Broadway just east of downtown San Diego. The apartment seemed big at the time, but as we look back now we realize it was quite tiny. I remember the bedroom would only take a three-quarter-sized bed. We ate off a cardboard bridge table that was so warped we had to hold our glasses of milk at dinner to keep them from falling over and spilling.

We had a couple of little stools that fit neatly under the card table so we could have more room to walk around in the tiny dining area off the kitchen. Just after we married we bought our first possessions, and they were brand new—a small refrigerator and a very small gas stove.

I'm not real sure what either cost, but I think the refrigerator was about $125 and the stove around $50. The rent I'd guess was around $35 a month. I know this much: you had to be pretty careful moving about or you'd run one another down. It was fun. Every couple remembers their first apartment or house, I guess. I used to be able to drive by and pick ours out, but I think now it's gone or my memory is, because the last time I was in the area I couldn't find it.

Although I had been working at Convair as a timekeeper I was in the throes of enlisting in the Navy. It seemed that every day I had to run somewhere to fill out another form or do something else.

We had known when we set the wedding for January 5 that I'd be going in very soon. Finally after what seemed weeks and a ton of paper work I was sworn in as an apprentice seaman on

January 27, 1951, just three weeks and a day after our wedding in La Jolla.

That meant boot camp for me. Since I'd been assigned to the Naval Training Center, we figured that it would be best if we moved out of the Broadway area apartment.

We found a little place in Pacific Beach on Diamond Street, but stayed only about three months or so when we found one on Hornblend we liked much better. Pacific Beach was much more convenient for Shirley's job at Convair and for me also.

I don't think we'll ever forget the place. The street wasn't paved and if a window was left open just a crack you had to dig your way into the house. The dust would be all over. Shirley's father had given us a vacuum cleaner as a wedding present and that little beauty went everyday just trying to stay even with the dust kicked up from the dirt road. It was really almost sand, very fine, and it got into everything.

This was a one-bedroom apartment. We had bought a little couch that made into a bed for the living room. We had a little wooden table and chairs that my dad had given to us along with an overstuffed chair. Shirley convinced me that I could recover it, and between the two of us we did—Shirley cutting the material while I did the tacking. I guess that was my first exposure to upholstery, but I've done a lot since, especially on cars.

I'd won a television set somewhere. It didn't work too well, but apprentice seamen had to get their entertainment where they could. I can remember going to the movies on the base many a night. It cost a dime each and they were pretty good movies—mostly first run.

Somewhere Shirley's mother had acquired some flour sacks made of printed muslin. Shirley spent hours making it into curtains for the apartment—cutting and ruffling and finishing it with turquoise trim. By the time she was done with the place it was kind of cute.

It was home, and we were happy. We lived there all the time I was in the Navy, more than three years.

I'll never forget the first time Shirley saw me after we got our first pass at boot camp. My hair couldn't have been much more than a quarter-inch long. I'd marched my feet off regular time and double time so I lost a little weight even though the food wasn't too bad and there was plenty to eat.

I hadn't seen anything of a golf club from the day I reported to the Naval Training Center reception area until I completed boot camp. Then I got orders assigning me to the Sail Ho golf course. It was part of the Naval Training Center grounds and was run by a wonderful old gentleman named Mike Vesock who must have been up around seventy at the time. He was primarily responsible for my getting in the program. The men assigned there helped him operate the golf course, run the driving range, give lessons, check out the clubs and any other chores that had to be done.

There really weren't too many lessons to give. Most of the time we just checked out clubs. Once in a while an officer or maybe an officer's wife would want a lesson, but it sure wasn't like a pro's job at a country club. We didn't wear blues but we wouldn't have won any prizes for best-dressed golfer either.

There were a lot of fine golfers on the base during my years —Billy Casper, Don Whitt, Frank Morey. My old friend Bud Holscher was among them too. Billy Casper came in about a year behind me and we played on the same team at the Naval Training Center.

Almost every military base in the state had a golf team. We played them and also a lot of the university teams—the University of Arizona, Stanford, Arizona State, places like that.

One year we played in the Interservice Championships at an Air Force base in Northern California, Hamilton Field, I think. Four of us—Frank Morey, Don Whitt, Billy Casper, and I—represented the Navy. We won the team title by about 26 strokes. Billy and I tied for first in the individual play and I beat him in a playoff.

After two years at the Training Center, I was transferred to the Naval Air Station on North Island. That's the part of Coronado Island where we used to bike as kids. I had to change my rating from seaman to airman because everyone attached to the station was subject to overseas duty. I drew overseas pay. That gave me something like four or five dollars more a month, and there I was, running a driving range.

That was my job. I gave lessons to enlisted men like myself, officers, and their wives, and I played on the station golf team. A good part of the day there wasn't much to do so I practiced a lot. I must have hit a million or so golf balls on that driving range.

It was during this time that I decided that once I was out of the Navy I was going to try the tour. Our enforced savings plan—living on my Navy pay and saving Shirley's income—was now the tour fund.

A big splurge for us would be to go out to dinner with the Holschers or some of the other people at the base. There was a place in Pacific Beach where you could get soup, salad, and entrée for 99 cents. For a dessert we'd go to an ice-cream parlor and buy a double-deck cone for a dime. That was our big night.

A big event in our young married life took place one Thanksgiving when I'd won a turkey at the driving range in the "turkey shoot." We'd invited Mom and her husband over for dinner. Shirley had never cooked a turkey before and I sure hadn't. The turkey weighed about twelve pounds and Shirley must have had twenty pounds of dressing stuffed in that bird. We ate turkey dressing for days afterwards.

There were a lot of restrictions in Navy life but I couldn't knock it. I spent my three plus years in San Diego and got to play a lot of golf. I met most of the captains and admirals in the area during those three years, gave some of them lessons, and, for a low-ranking airman, lived a pretty nice life.

Littler, Gene A., 4257102, Am. USN—that was my official roster title the last two years in the Navy. I probably remember my final days in the Navy best of all. I was due to be discharged February 2, 1954.

I had accumulated some leave time and had made a request for either seven or ten days' leave so I could enter the San Diego Open. It was actually called the Convair San Diego Open and was played at the Rancho Santa Fe course. Billy Casper and I were both in it against all the top tour pros of the day—Dutch Harrison, Cary Middlecoff, Jimmy Demaret, Lloyd Mangrum, Lew Worsham, Ted Kroll, Tommy Bolt, Julius Boros, Ed Furgol, to name a few.

It started on a Thursday, and Billy and I had played a few practice rounds before. I went out that day and shot a super round of 67—and darned if it didn't hold up as the first-round lead by two strokes. I remember the papers saying that "Gene Littler, the Navy airman, was leading the best of the pros at the end of the first round." They seemed to be implying that I wouldn't be doing that after the second round.

I surprised them and I guess myself by doing even better the next eighteen. I shot a 66 to give me a 133, three strokes ahead of Dutch Harrison who had shot 69–67 and who was just coming off winning $2,000 first prize money by a shot from Demaret in the Bing Crosby the week before.

I was hot. There was no doubt about it. All that practice and play in the Navy was standing up well. Every time I looked around at the gallery that was following us I would see an officer, an officer's wife or some of the guys from the Air Station. But I didn't panic. I shot a 69 in the third round and held a five-stroke lead at 202 over Harrison and Middlecoff at 207.

Then it started to rain on the final round. It was Sunday and it came down and it came down. We were delayed for a while but somehow we got all the field in. I felt mighty fortunate to shoot a 72 in that kind of weather. Harrison shot a 71 and Middlecoff a 73.

My 274 won the tournament, one of the big wins of my amateur career. It also qualified me for my first Tournament of Champions. Harrison took top money of $2,400 at 278 and Dr. Cary tied with Ted Kroll at 280 for $1,600 each.

For me the prize was a silver service: you know, a sterling silver coffee pot, creamer and sugar bowl. We still have that, and it is one of our prized possessions. I remember that Esther Williams presented it to me and gave Harrison his check. We still use the silver service but I'm sure that Dutch has long since spent the $2,400.

The money seemed like a lot that day in 1954 to a golfer who was playing for the experience but just the same this Navy man was mighty happy and mighty proud. I'd played with the best of them and won.

12

There wasn't too much more to accomplish in amateur golf. I'd been fortunate the year before (while still in the Navy and again on leave) to have won the 1953 U.S. National Amateur title in Oklahoma City. I had played on the victorious United States Walker Cup team just before that tournament, so there were only six days available for practice at the Oklahoma Golf and Country Club.

Since the National Amateur was a match play affair, a bad round or a few bad holes could mean you'd be out. I really didn't give much thought to winning the tournament until I got into the semifinals. Once play went to thirty-six holes—which it did in the semifinals and finals—I felt I had a good chance. I was in great shape, thanks to the Navy, and my game was especially strong after the Walker Cup matches.

I beat Bruce Cudd in the semifinals and after twenty-seven holes things looked awfully rosy in the finals against Dale Morey. I was leading by three up with nine to go. Suddenly I sort of went to sleep as I had a couple of chances to really put him away and get it over at the 12th and 15th holes. Then Dale knocked in two good putts. Things looked pretty bleak as we approached the final fairway all even.

I thought of only one thing after we hit our tee shots. I remembered the time Mac Hunter beat me in the finals of the California Amateur on the 39th hole. Golly, I thought, I hope this isn't going to be the Hunter match all over again.

I was on the green, finally, about fifteen feet above the hole. Morey helped me a bit by hitting his second shot into a trap and not coming out too well. He was eight or ten feet away.

Once again I felt I couldn't lose the hole, especially with Dale that far away. It looked as though two putts might win the hole, but I had to try to make it. As I got down to read the green, the hole looked smaller than a dime and shrinking. And was it quiet. It was almost spooky how quiet since we had a gallery of about five thousand.

Noise has never bothered me. When I get ready to hit the ball, I don't hear a thing or see the gallery. The jangling of a key ring or some one coughing or a photographer shooting his camera seldom bothers me. The thing that bothers me most in a situation like this is my own breathing.

So, as I studied the break of the green, the fifteen- to eighteen-foot distance to the hole, the cup just seemed to get smaller. I got up and lined up the putt. My mallet-head putter seemed pretty heavy, but as I stroked the ball it made a nice, perfect curling run into the cup.

I remember I just dropped the putter on the green and said to myself, "Well, that's it. Thank goodness."

Then it seemed like all five thousand in the gallery surrounded me. Shirley, who was carrying Curt at the time, finally got next to me, and it was one of the most joyous moments of our young lives. Next day the papers pointed out that I was the third youngest player ever to win the amateur. Francis Ouimet was twenty-one back in 1914, Bobby Jones was twenty-one in 1924, and Billy Maxwell was the same age as I—twenty-three —when he won in 1951.

As we walked toward the clubhouse some youngster came up and congratulated me. In my hand I had the ball I holed out with. I offered it to him but he refused. He told me I should keep it as a trophy of the 53rd U.S. Amateur. For several days

I didn't know what had happened to it but when we got home I found it in the slacks I wore.

It was a wonderful win. I remember one of the sports writers asking: "Any visions of turning pro?"

"I've thought a little bit about it," I said, "but that's about it. I've still got about six months to go in the Navy."

That seed must have been growing in our minds. After winning the San Diego Open at Rancho Santa Fe it appeared now was the hour to try the tour.

Actually we didn't base the decision solely on the San Diego Open win. I feel it was a culmination of several things—my selection to the Walker Cup team, winning the United States Amateur, the California State Amateur championship and finally beating the best of the pros in the San Diego Open.

Thanks to Shirley's saving all she had earned we had about $9,000 as a sort of bankroll to put us on tour.

I remember a letter I had received from Bing Crosby the morning of the San Diego Open. I had first been invited to his "clambake"—as he called it—two years before. When I opened his letter dated January 20, 1954, I thought back to the Crosby tournament the week before that Dutch Harrison had won.

Four of us had tied for low amateur with our partners— Harvey Ward, Jr.; Lefty O'Doul, the famous baseball player; Monty Moncrief; and I.

"With the four amateurs tying for first place," Bing wrote, "in the Amateur-Pro Division, we had to have a draw to see who got first and second prizes. They are all watches, but the first and second prizes are a little better than the other two. Hate to give you the bad news that Harvey Ward won the draw and Moncrief was second, but I hope that when the watch does go to you that you will like it all right."

Then he added a prophetic postcript: "I will be pulling for you to have some real good rounds in the San Diego Open, and I look forward to seeing you again some day and maybe playing when I am in a little better shape."

Three days after winning the San Diego Open we made the announcement during the Calcutta dinner for the Thunderbird

Invitational at Thunderbird Country Club in Palm Springs. I would join the pro tour. That was January 27, 1954, and under the regulations of the Professional Golfers Association, I was not going to be eligible for money in sanctioned events until my six months' probationary period expired.

Shortly after we decided to make the big jump a lot of things happened. Thanks to John Dawson, one of the great amateur golfers of all time, I signed a contract with the Thunderbird Country Club to play out of their club. The next day or so I signed with Spalding to use their equipment—with another Dawson, John's brother George, who then was a vice-president of Spalding.

It all seemed unreal when I teed up for the Thunderbird. What seemed like only hours ago, I was an airman in the Navy and an amateur. Now I was a pro setting out to go head and head with the big guns of golf like Ben Hogan, Jackie Burke, Lloyd Mangrum, Jimmy Demaret, Byron Nelson—all the people I had dreamed about as a kid.

I continued to play well, shooting 68–68–71–68—275. That would have earned me $262.50, but since I was serving my apprenticeship all I got was thanks.

Nearly a month passed before I entered my second tournament but the days flew by. We were frantically getting ready to hit the road. I'd be discharged. We had taken delivery of the car trailer that Thunderbird Country Club had bought us and a new Mercury sedan to pull it with.

I knew nothing about pulling a trailer. And you can imagine what I knew about getting a trailer hitch put on a car, rigging the turn lights so they worked, and most of all trying to back that big thing into a stall in a trailer park. I always thought I was pretty good with a car but when you saddle one with a big old boxcar-like addition it is something else.

There were some nonsanctioned tournaments around where an apprentice professional could accept prize money. The Mexican National Open was one and I entered that late in February and won $145, hardly air fare down and back, and my scores of 74–71–73–76—294 were not the greatest.

My next stop was the Masters. I'd dreamed of playing in it

for years. I had been invited in 1953 by Mr. Clifford Roberts, chairman of the Masters Tournament Committee, but I had other commitments—mainly the Navy—and had to pass it up.

This year, on April 8, 1954, I entered my first Masters. I had seen the course on television, with its huge, wide fairways, beautiful trees, and large greens, but nothing will ever replace the thrill of my first practice round. I just felt that I was the luckiest young golfer in the world.

I finished 22nd with rounds of 79–75–73–72—299 and won $442.86. That's the Masters where Sam Snead and Ben Hogan ended up in a tie at 289 and Snead shot a 70 to Hogan's 71 to win the 18-hole playoff and $5,000 first-prize money.

No sooner had I got back to San Diego than Shirley and I began to pack everything in the trailer preparatory to starting a trailer trek on the circuit. What we couldn't take in the trailer we stored with one of our parents.

Curt Michael Littler had been born March 11, 1954, in Mercy Hospital. The little guy was just past a month old when we loaded him and all his paraphernalia into the trailer or the car. I had gone out on some practice spins with the trailer. I did just great going straight ahead. I wasn't too bad on the turns. But backing up was something else. You were blind, almost, and about the only way I could really maneuver the thing was with Shirley on the outside coaching.

Our first tour stop was going to be the Tournament of Champions at the Desert Inn Country Club in Las Vegas. It was the second richest stop on the tour at $35,000. The Masters was worth $33,500 with the number one event being the World Championship of Golf put on by George May at the Tam O'Shanter Country Club outside of Chicago. It was worth $99,999.87. Don't ask me why the 87 cents, but that was the total prize money.

We left La Jolla early one morning with Las Vegas our destination. We got initiated into the precarious ways of hauling a trailer almost the first day. Here we were, brand-new parents, on our first golf tour, pulling a trailer with all our possessions back behind. We were about half way between nowhere and noplace, when we blew a tire on the trailer. I can't remember why the spare wouldn't work, but it wouldn't. So Shirley and Curt stayed in the trailer and I had to drive about sixty miles each way to get a new tire. I wasn't for leaving Shirley and Curt alone, but she insisted someone had to stay with our possessions, so off I went.

We were an awfully happy young couple after the first tournament. I finished with a 289 which was 11 strokes back of Art Wall, Jr.'s 278. That earned him $10,000; my 289 was a tie for seventh for $1,000, which seemed like a lot of money at the time.

We got a little more baptism driving the trailer from Las Vegas to San Francisco. We had a series of blowouts that made me begin to suspect that the tires just weren't heavy enough for the job, so we decided to leave the trailer in the middle of Nevada somewhere and drive on over to San Francisco for the $10,000 San Francisco Pro-Am at Lake Merced Golf Club.

I finished in a tie for fourth with Smiley Quick, a Southern California golfer I'd played against ever since I was a kid. We each shot 217, good for $600 behind Shelly Mayfield's 212 and $1,400 first-prize money. Shirley and I thought we had found the money machine. Here in our first two tournaments we had won $1,600. That looked like an absolute fortune to two kids who had been used to getting by on a Navy airman's pay of less than $100 per month.

Now our trailer tour began in earnest. We weren't alone in living the trailer life. The Billy Caspers and the Bud Holschers had trailers. So did the Doug Fords and the Dick Mayers. Heading east from Nevada, our next tour stop was the Palm Beach Round Robin Invitational at the Meadow Brook Club on Long Island.

We had decided to drive to Cincinnati (site of the Western Open the first week in June), park the trailer, and drive to New York for the Round Robin. Planning is easy but real execution is something else.

Two or three more blowouts confirmed my opinion that the tires just weren't heavy enough for the weight of the trailer. It seemed as if we were switching tires about every fifty miles or so. I know that wasn't the case but it sure seemed like it every time I had to jack up that heavy trailer.

Somewhere between Chicago and Cincinnati—I vaguely recall it was near Fort Wayne, Indiana—we had a real problem. We were coming up a long hill, and just as I ducked over the top, this big truck came winging west like he was late for the start of the Indianapolis 500. The wind was blowing us around a bit and I couldn't keep the car and the trailer on our side of the two-lane road. I had to run off the road and through a farmer's fence, flipping the trailer over on its side and snapping off the tongue.

Curt was asleep in the back seat of the light blue Merc. We were terrified that he was hurt but he didn't even wake up. We were fortunate that the car didn't roll. We had to get the farmer to help us right the trailer and we had to pay him for the damage to his fence poles and barbed wire. In all, over about fifteen or eighteen months, we tried three trailers, but we finally just gave up on the idea.

Trailer living was great but hauling the things was something else. We went from the 27- to a 33-foot job and then back down to a 21-foot one, but I never could find the combination that seemed right.

We had a lot of fun. Often several of the other tour players would end up with us in the same trailer park. This gave the gals someone to talk with and a chance to share baby-sitting chores if they needed to go shopping, to see a doctor or something.

You couldn't beat the cost. We paid $1 or at the most $2 per night to park, and Shirley cooked most of our meals which made living fairly cheap. Our heaviest expenses were for the auto and caddie fees.

The trailer life didn't seem to bother my golf game. I finished ninth in the Round Robin, winning $650. Then I was twelfth in the Colonial National Invitational in Fort Worth, where I picked up $708.33, and was fifth in the Western Open for another $833.33.

While I didn't win a tour event for dollars that year, I

finished second in four tournaments and won a total officially of $8,327.50. Actually, my total winnings in 1954 were $16,306.52. Most important, we never dipped into the savings that Shirley had saved so carefully those three plus years in the Navy.

Of all the showings I made the first year the greatest came in what I believe is the toughest test of professional golf—the United States Open, June 17–19, 1954, at Baltusrol Country Club in Springfield, New Jersey.

I had gone to Baltusrol a week early, passing up the Virginia Beach Open in order to practice and get as ready as possible. In those days the U.S. Open was a three-day tournament with a 36-hole final the last day. On any golf course that is a test, but especially so in the Open with all the pressure, the big galleries, and the outstanding golfers you have to face.

This was no exception. Ben Hogan was after his fifth U.S. Open title, and he too had come ahead of time to prepare, though from all I could see he was ready. About four months before I was hitting balls on the driving range at North Island Naval Air Station and working in games on courses around San Diego.

Here I was with the legends—Hogan, Snead, Locke, Mangrum, Demaret—a kid trying on big shoes in the toughest test there was. I went out on the opening round and shot a 70 that put me in second place with Ted Kroll, one shot back of one of my old amateur rivals, Billy Joe Patton, the leader with a 69.

I went back to our trailer feeling great but also well aware that it would be difficult to win the Open the first time I tried. But on the second day I shot a 69 to give me a 139 total and the lead. That left me almost speechless.

I had trouble in the morning round of the final day, shooting a six-over 76 and surrendering the lead to Ed Furgol. I missed a few fairways and the rough was pretty tough, which made it difficult to score.

There was some consolation with the round, however, since Ben Hogan who also was struggling had 76. Now, however, we had to turn right around and go the final 18. I was young, and a little upset, but I knew I needed a good final round to be in contention.

When you're a month and two days away from your twenty-fourth birthday, reality suddenly overtakes you along the way and you wonder just what in the world you're doing in this competition, playing in the U.S. Open and having a shot at the championship.

But I forced all those thoughts out of my mind, grabbed a quick soft drink, a bite to eat on the run, and went out to do my best. You can always fault yourself no matter how well you do, but when I came up to the 18th green looking at an eight-foot putt to tie Furgol for the title and force a playoff, I was really nervous. I was about to try to make an eight-footer for the one championship every player dreams of winning.

A birdie would give me a 69 and a 284 total. I looked that putt over from every angle, and as I gathered myself together, testing the swing of my putter, the biggest noise around came from my own breath going in and out.

I had arrived at the green the hard way. My tee shot couldn't have been better, a long one right down the middle of the fairway packed with 15,000 people. I tried to hit a fade with a four-wood to reach this par-5 hole. The ball stayed straight and caught the left trap. I left my sand shot eight feet above the hole, which meant quite a tricky downhill putt on a surface as fast as glass.

There was nothing wrong with the putt except it was a bit strong. It caressed the edge of the cup, ran past it two feet, and the title was Furgol's. I won $3,600, the most money I had ever seen in one lump sum.

Naturally, I was disappointed. I had come within a blade of grass or two of maybe winning the Open in the same year I had won the U.S. Amateur. No one had done that since Bobby Jones.

Thinking back on it at the time, I could see a hundred ways I could have won the tournament. I was disappointed but not dissatisfied.

When I had arrived at Baltusrol the week before, I had hoped I might finish in the first ten so I wouldn't have to qualify the next year. Then I looked over the scoreboard. I was four shots ahead of Ben Hogan, five up on Sam Snead, one up on Lloyd Mangrum, three up on Bobby Locke. That was pretty good company to be ahead of, plus all the other great golfers who had played.

Frankly, I had not felt too much pressure from the time I began the tour in Las Vegas in April, but it all converged on me at the Open. I really felt it on that last putt. Still, it was a remarkable run at the national title. And when the 1954 tour ended the third week in September with the National Celebrities Open at the Congressional Country Club in Washington D.C., I had to be more than satisfied, especially since I was the 28th leading money winner for about half of the swing.

There were many things that made our long drive back to La Jolla a satisfying one, even with the task of towing that big, old trailer. But one of the best was a remark Gene Sarazen made: "Gene Littler is the finest prospect in golf."

A smiling Gene Littler introduces his son, Curt, 19, after the St. Louis Children's Hospital Golf Classic July 23, 1973—Gene's first victory since undergoing cancer surgery in April 1972. Winner's trophy can be seen in left foreground. (Wide World Photo)

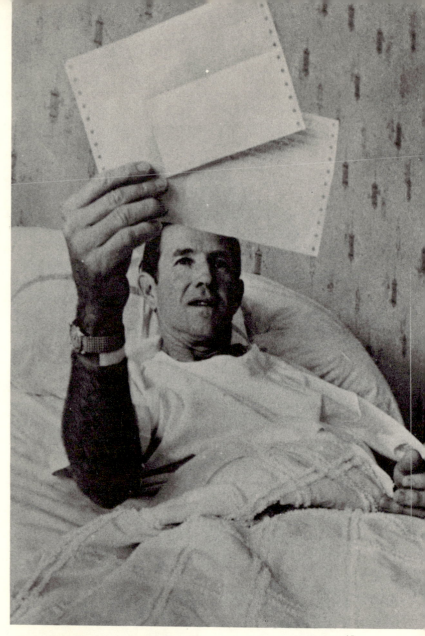

In the hospital after successful cancer surgery, Gene reads "get well" telegrams. (Wide World Photo)

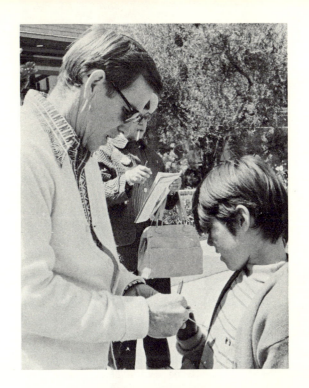

16 days after surgery
Gene signs auto-
graph for young fan
at Rancho La Costa
Country Club during
1972 Tournament
of Champions. Gene
had qualified for
this event but could
not participate.
(Joe Flynn photo)

A paint job on Shirley's Rolls occupies Gene as he recuperates. (Wide·
World Photo)

Left: Jack Littler gives 2-year-old brother Gene a bite of his apple. Right: 4-year-old cowboy Gene astride Black Beauty.

Family orchestra session: Gene, 9, is on violin; Jack, 11, trumpet; Dick, 15, piano; father plays cello and mother, accordion.

Above: Gene as student at San Diego State College in 1950, with his well-groomed 1941 Ford coupe.

At La Jolla Country Club, Gene practices during high school days, wearing typical "uniform" of un-pressed corduroys with turned-up cuffs.

1950 San Diego State College golf team on the practice tee. Left to right: Bill Hurlburt, Frank Morey, Jr., Lloyd Schunemann, Gene Littler.

January 5, 1951. Gene and Shirley cut their wedding cake at reception at La Jolla Country Club following ceremony.

Above: Gene holds son Curt for picture after christening ceremony at Christ Lutheran Church in Pacific Beach. Left to right are Dr. Bob Lowry; Gene's mother; Shirley; the Reverend Quentin Garman; Curt and Gene; Mrs. Warren.

Gene and Shirley arrive in San Diego following Gene's win of U.S. Amateur golf championship September 1953 in Oklahoma City.

Gene holds silver service given to him by actress Esther Williams for winning the Convair San Diego Open in 1954 at Rancho Santa Fe Country Club. E. J. (Dutch) Harrison, left, finished second but took first-prize money for pros. Between Miss Williams and Littler is Ben Gage, then Miss Williams's husband.

Gene checks trailer hitch as he prepares to park during the Houston Open in 1955, the first full season in his long professional career.

Jubilant Nan and Frankie Laine buss Gene after first of his three successive Tournament of Champion wins at Desert Inn in Las Vegas.

Comedian Bob Hope, an able golfer in his own right, pauses to give counsel to Bud Holscher (left) and Gene Littler during a tournament in California.

The late Bobby Jones (right), known in his heyday as Emperor of Golf, chats with Mr. and Mrs. Gene Littler during 1959 Masters at Augusta National. (Bill Mark photo)

13

Out on tour, especially in our early years when we were a trailer tribe and driving as much as fifteen hundred miles between playing sites, we had little time for anything but golf. It wasn't until I was home and going through some back newspapers our parents had saved that I fully realized how wonderful some of the truly great stars of golf had been to me.

I had seen Gene Sarazen's remark in the east but I had sure missed some of the others. And as I read them I wondered aloud who they were talking about, because the Gene Littler they were talking about wasn't the Gene Littler I thought I knew.

Ben Hogan, whom I probably admired more than anyone in golf because of what he had done after his horrible accident, said I was the best of the young prospects. "Littler has two great assets," he said, "in big, strong hands and wrists like wagon tongues." Until then I had never paid much attention to wagon tongues.

Jimmy Demaret, another class guy and close friend of Hogan's, paid me a super compliment. "I don't think there has ever been anybody to match Hogan," said Demaret, "but Littler is the nearest thing to him I've seen in years. He has the same slide rule mind."

Now, Jimmy may know a lot about my golf, but he wasn't too familiar with my academic achievements. I always had trouble with a slide rule, although I do feel that I am pretty number-oriented and enjoy some of the elementary aspects of math.

Fred Corcoran, who really gave professional golf a tremendous lift when he was tournament director of the PGA, climbed out on a limb that was mighty slim. He said I was the next Bobby Jones.

Wow. That's a lot to measure up to, and here I had played not quite half a year on the tour. "In all my years," said Corcoran, "I've seen few players come along with the natural ability of Littler. He has everything: poise, skill and is the personification of confidence. Littler has come into the professional field as the finest prospect in years."

Grantland Rice, probably the most famous sportswriter of his time, was extremely kind, calling me the "most promising golfer" to come along. "Littler is what you might call a stylist," wrote Rice. "His body, head, and hands are at the right spot at the moment of impact."

Then he hedged his bet, and he was probably the first man to call this shot. "Whether he has the capacity for long hard work that Hogan and Nelson have remains to be seen."

Some will no doubt point to this and say it is the flaw in Gene Littler's game. Perhaps they are accurate. Perhaps they are not.

I feel I have the capacity for the hard work it takes to play top-level professional golf. What I was not willing to do—to pay the price, as they say—was stay out on the tour away from my family week after week.

In the early years when we pulled the trailer and after that when we just drove, I paid the price. I made most of the tournaments. But when Curt began school and Shirley had to stay home my whole perspective of golf changed.

I was just not willing to go out week after week for six or

seven months. I decided then that I'd play in two or three tournaments and then pass up one or two to return to my family. From the standpoint of competition that probably is a mistake. It takes a week or two and sometimes three to get into the pace of things—the groove, as some call it.

But in two weeks or three at the most, I would head home. After a week or two around the house doing a little practicing but spending most of the time with my family and working on my cars, I'd go out again. It was like starting all over.

Often it was frustrating because I knew there were many cases where I'd do better if I stayed out. But here I was at home. Yet home was where I wanted to be. I still feel that way although now that Curt and Suzy are both out of high school I may stay out a little longer at a time with Shirley along.

You don't give yourself your best chance going back and forth. When I didn't play well, I'd get really torn between the two things. Obviously, I preferred being home because my family always meant more to me than golf, but yet it was impossible to ignore the fact that I wasn't playing as well as I knew I could and as people expected me to.

When I began in 1954 the separation really never entered my mind because I knew that Shirley and Curt, and later Suzanne, would be with me. Then when school came into the picture it suddenly dawned on me that I was going to be out there alone. That I didn't like. That's when I made the decision to split the tour with time at home.

Grantland Rice was a prophet after all. I had the capacity for the hard work but not the capacity to be away from my wife and children week after week. Maybe I shouldn't have split the time so evenly—perhaps it would have been better to go out for four or five weeks and then take two weeks off. I don't know. All I do know is that if I could do it all over again, I wouldn't change. My family is first, always. Golf has to be second.

Really, I guess what I am is just a quiet personality who likes to be with those closest to him and to enjoy all the things he can have at home. For me that means a monkey wrench and an old car, and to have this and be able to play golf for a living I feel very fortunate.

That's why one of the by-products of winning golf is so hard for me, and for some of the people on the other end of it, the writers. I'm talking about press area interviews. I'm not a very gregarious, happy-go-lucky individual like an Arnold Palmer or a Chi Chi Rodriguez or a Lee Trevino, so consequently I'm sure I must rank up there with those the press rate as "poor interviews." Sometimes I wish I could be one of those very, very colorful golfers, but I am not, and I just hope all those who do such a tremendous job of making golf such a widely accepted game will understand me a little better.

It's always been my nature not to elaborate much on things, not get too carried away. If I go out and shoot a couple of 78s in the next tournament there won't be many around to talk to me. So I've tried to keep things in perspective, to keep my modesty and be as unassuming as possible. I've found out making three straight birdies is nothing to get excited about because you might bogey the next four holes.

I try to cooperate, to answer all the questions, but as a lot of the media people know, they'd better grab me fast because I'm on a one-way road to the clubhouse and a shower. All I want to do, hopefully, is play a good game of golf, conduct myself in a sportsmanlike manner, and get back to my family.

For years before he died, my dad urged me to have great confidence in myself and to appreciate the interest in my ability as a golfer and the fact that the people in the gallery and the press truly did want to be close to me. Maybe the real truth is that I'm a little nervous before all those cameras, microphones, and pencils.

There's no doubt I've made certain aspects of this game harder than they are. Golf is not a game of great shots. It's a game of the most accurate misses. Those who win make the fewest errors.

Golf is a great game, and it takes some of all kinds to make it so. Thanks to golf, I've been very fortunate in life. I'm trying to put a bit more back into it now and I hope maybe even a little more in the future.

Something that had always intrigued me but I didn't know until we did some in-depth research for this book was who had hung the name "Gene the Machine" on me. I knew some sports-writer had written it but every time I was asked I had to plead ignorance. I'm sure many a writer wondered just why I couldn't remember. But in all honesty it was only after going through old newspaper files that I discovered it was Earl Keller, a San Diego sportswriter and longtime friend who has written con-siderably about me for many years. He wrote that line in 1953 during the California State Open at Rancho Santa Fe, when I was still in the Navy and still an amateur. "Littler gained a new nickname, 'The Machine.' He played like one. His card showed fourteen pars and four birdies. Gene hit something like 16 greens in regulation figures and if he had any more luck with his putts he would have shot a 64."

I'd forgotten all about that tournament even though I won it. I shot a first-round 68, then three consecutive 71s for a 281. Babe Lazane from Bakersfield was second at 286; Harry Cooper and Jack Gage tied for third.

I've never considered myself a machine although I'm pretty good at fixing up auto machines. But every once in a while that line would crop up in a story and until now I'd always wonder where it came from. I guess I owe Earl Keller an apology for my bad memory.

14 O━O━O━O━O━O━O━O━O

With the beginning of the New Year in 1955 we had traded trailers—stepped up to a 33-footer with a two-tone green Nash Ambassador to do the pulling. Only thing I can remember about that setup was that the car had a great deal of play in the steering wheel and you really had to work at pulling the trailer.

This was my first full shot at the tour and I made most of the major events. There were a total of forty-nine tournaments of all kinds. I entered and won something in thirty-two as we trundled around the countryside always looking ahead for a trailer park to set down in for a week.

Our first stop was the Los Angeles Open. It was the first event of the winter swing and was played in 1955 at the Inglewood Country Club, a unique course. Unfortunately, like so many others, it has since given way to a housing project.

I had only played in the Los Angeles Open twice before, the last time being in 1949. After the first round when I trailed Bo Winninger's lead 68 by four, I was really afraid of only one man. That was me. Out on a golf course the chief threat is you. Beat yourself and the others don't have to.

And this time out I didn't beat myself. I was not too happy

with my opening one-over-par 72, but then I put together rounds of 67–68–69 for a 276—two strokes ahead of Ted Kroll —and my first win on the tour as a pro. I'll never forget that course. Every time you looked up you were staring down at an oil well pumping up and down.

It was a big win for me. Worth $5,000, the most I'd ever seen in one check and surely a great way to start a new year. There was only one thing wrong. Shirley wasn't there for the final round. Curt, who was ten months old at the time, had become ill and she had gone back to San Diego. It was still eighteen days short of my first anniversary as a pro and things looked awfully bright.

What really set up the win on the final round was my approach shot on 16. I was about sixty feet out and my chip was like an arrow going straight and true and into the cup on the 215-yard hole for a birdie two. That shot, probably more than any other, clinched the win for me and started me on a year in which I eventually ended up fifth in official money winnings at $28,974.42.

Not only did the Los Angeles Open give me my biggest winnings ever but it also guaranteed me another $1,000. Every winner of a sanctioned event was qualified to play in the Tournament of Champions in Las Vegas. At that time the tour ended in September or the first week in October and the Tournament of Champions was the last weekend in April.

The tour didn't have the geographic continuity it does now, so by time for us to head for Las Vegas, we had crisscrossed the United States up and down and back and forth playing in twelve tournaments and accumulating winnings of $12,463.26. The Tournament of Champions had begun in 1953, and all the pros liked it since it was a guaranteed $1,000 no matter where you finished.

It kind of took the dollar pressure off a player. In those days my objective was to win $1,000 or more each week. If we could win in four figures, we felt we were in good shape financially.

Some people called the Tournament of Champions the Littler Benefit for a while.

It all began in 1955, maybe as we were driving to Las Vegas

from San Diego. Frankie Laine, the famous singer, and his wife, Nan, were driving to Las Vegas so Frankie could be one of the auctioneers in the Calcutta, a kind of pool where golfers were sold to the highest bidder and the proceeds distributed at the end of the tournament according to a prearranged formula. Now Calcuttas are illegal but they were quite common at tournaments then and in some club championships around the country.

A portion of the price paid for participants in the Tournament of Champions went to the Damon Runyon Cancer Fund. It was 10 percent as I recall, and the idea was created by the late Walter Winchell, a lifelong friend of Runyon's.

As the Laines were driving from their Beverly Hills home, Nan was reading a paper and saw a picture of me. The way Frankie told it to me later she thought that if he was going to handle some of the auction he should at least bid on one of the players, and she liked my looks.

"I'm a Sunday hacker who shoots 95, not counting the misses," Laine told *Sports Illustrated.* "I didn't know a Calcutta pool from a Bombay duck." Laine figured that players went for $200 or $300 and the fact that I was registered out of Thunderbird in Palm Springs led him to believe I must know something about playing a desert course.

The opening bid on me was $10,000 by Morris Kleinman, a prominent Las Vegas figure who was sitting with Laine. Up popped Laine to bid $10,500. Some of his friends sitting with him wondered if he was ready for the booby hatch. The bidding went back and forth, and before Frankie knew it the gavel came down and he had bid $13,000, considerably more than the $200 or $300 Nan thought I would go for.

Up until then I had never met Frankie Laine. Sure, I was aware of him, especially his rendition of "Mule Train," "That's My Desire," and "Lucky Old Sun," which I liked a lot.

I understand he hedged just a bit, selling off 25 percent to a San Francisco oil man, Chauncey Needham, and another 25 percent to a friend from Beverly Hills, Don Frankel.

We were playing the Desert Inn course. I tied for the lead in the first round with 69 and just seemed to get hotter as the rounds rolled by. I remember going into the final round ten strokes up on the field. Frankie Laine was walking on air. So were we. First prize was $10,000 out of the $35,000 purse.

The morning of the final round, I ran into Frankie going out to the practice tee. Some Las Vegas type had just offered to buy him out of the Calcutta for $70,000. The winner would only bring $72,500.

"I'm this far," Frankie told him, "I'll stay to the end."

The end found me a winner by 13 strokes over Pete Cooper, Jerry Barber and Bob Toski, who all tied at 293 and won $2566 each.

My check for $10,000 looked mighty large and I was especially proud of the way I'd played. It was probably the best four rounds of golf I ever played, and to win by 13 strokes was one of the largest margins of victory ever, for anyone.

That final day I only had one worry. Finishing. I was worried I might break a leg or might not be able to finish for some physical reason. I was eight under par for the tournament—a record at the time.

The next year the price went up and Laine was forced up to $16,500. Like many other people, Frankie tried to do everything exactly the same way as in 1955, staying in the same room, wearing the same clothes, even going to bed at the precise hour of 2:40 A.M. after reading the chapter from Dr. Norman Vincent Peale's *The Power of Positive Thinking* entitled "Expect the Best and Get It."

I'll never forget walking to the first tee at the Desert Inn. Frankie repeated his positive thought of the previous year. "Each time you bring down that club, say to yourself, 'I believe.'"

I laughed. It loosened me up just as it had the first time. I wasn't too far off my game of 1955, winning again with a 281. Only this time Dr. Cary Middlecoff was only four strokes behind me at 285 and took the $4,000 second-place money alone.

But from my win at Las Vegas in 1956 until my return in 1957—defending champions were automatically eligible—I went through the worst siege in my golf career. I didn't win a single tournament. But despite my record going in—30th, 20th,

20th, 20th, 34th, 29th, 10th, 8th, and 44th—the price in the Calcutta was still $15,000 and Frankie was the high bidder.

I told him several times not even to bid for me because everything was going wrong. I felt there was no sense in wasting his money because he wasn't going to get a dime back. I'd been in eleven tournaments until the Tournament of Champions—it was played April 26–29—and in the money in nine but my total winnings of $1,998.50 had hardly paid my entry and caddy fees.

Everyone had a different theory on what was wrong with my game. I had a new one almost every day. One told me I had a loop at the top of my swing. Someone else said my right hand was too dominant. Another that my stance was too open.

All I know was that my game was terrible. And there didn't seem to be much I could do about it. When I went 73–73 in the first two rounds everyone wrote me off and I'm sure Frankie was among them, although he put up a good front. Then the winds came up on round three and all of a sudden my game seemed to blow together with the desert breeze. I shot a 69— one of the few sub-par rounds I had been able to shoot all year. It was good for a one-stroke lead. On the final day I shot a 70. That was good enough for a three-stroke victory and a third straight Tournament of Champions.

Looking back, my Tournament of Champions record stands out as one of my major achievements. When you talk about major championships—the Open, the Masters, the British and the PGA—every one of the men winning them was in the Tournament of Champions field each year and I beat them all three years in a row.

There were two more tournaments played with the Calcutta before they were banned. I tied for fourth in 1958 with 281 and the final year I was third.

Frankie told me one time that altogether they had invested $65,000 in me and grossed $263,000, ending up ahead $198,000. With his winnings he built what he called The Littler Room onto his home. It was a large playroom of perhaps 1500 square feet with terazzo floors, an indoor barbecue, hi-fi, piano, projection equipment, and a huge juke box.

Above the piano was a large glass trophy case. Frankie called it "The Gene Littler Shrine." It was lined with red velvet and held little mementoes from our wins such as tees, scorecards, and sun visors. He even had the golf balls gold plated.

Frankie now lives in San Diego and I see him once in a while. He and Nan are super people. He was sure kind to me. He gave me a 1957 Thunderbird after the third year and always gave me a percentage of his winnings.

When we reminisce about that remarkable three year run, one story always comes to mind. Curt was still just a tyke and one of our longtime friends, Dr. John Moler, a dentist, had come up for the tournament. I'm sure John had a little wager on me, and this particular morning we were all going out of the hotel together. I had my putter with me because I used to take it up to our room and do a little practicing on the rug.

As we were walking across the parking lot, Doc noticed that Curt was dragging my putter along the sidewalk and across the parking lot. Here Doc has probably bet what he considers a lot of money on me in the tournament and Curt is dragging along one of the most important clubs of all. Finally, he couldn't stand it any longer. He reached down and took the putter away from Curt, explaining to him, "That putter is mighty important to your daddy's golf game."

Frankie had one saying that he used all during this run: "You can't beat the three L's."

When someone would ask what the third L was he'd say, "Littler, Laine and the Lord."

But the way my golf game was going in 1957—even with the win in the Tournament of Champions—I wondered often just where the Lord stood! Discounting my $10,000 from Las Vegas I won only $13,427, and that won't keep you on tour very long.

15

After almost three disastrous years—1956, 1957, and 1958—I decided in November of 1958 that I had to do something. I elected to pass up the Florida portion of the tour that winter and remain in La Jolla to try and work out my problems.

Golf had always been an uncomplicated game for me. I just stepped up to the ball and swung. It was almost too simple. That's what made my collapse such a disaster.

Nothing I did worked, and I tried everything. Almost any suggestion I'd hear I would try, but still I couldn't find my game. It's hard to explain, and perhaps there is no explanation. I was like an airplane pilot who knew nothing about the plane except how to fly it. When the engine conked out he didn't have the slightest idea how to fix it and get it going again.

That was Gene Littler in November 1958.

That's when I went to Paul Runyan, then the professional at La Jolla Country Club. He had known me since about 1950, and rather intimately since 1955, when he took over as the pro at our club.

"Look," I said to him, "I'm a spastic or something. Help."

That's when he told me that a year before while I was practicing on the driving range he realized my swing was full of problems. He hadn't said anything to me because it had always been his policy that a professional of tour caliber had to realize his problem and voluntarily ask for assistance.

My appeal for help may not have been a scream but it was close to it.

We went out on the practice tee at La Jolla and I hit a few balls as Paul watched. After a few minutes he stopped me.

"Gene, you have your right hand too far under the shaft," I recall his telling me. He showed me how I was gripping the club wrong. "Put your right hand more on top of the shaft and then you won't close the clubface on the backswing and make your swing so flat."

I went from a strong grip to one more on top of the club. I moved my hands perhaps a quarter of a turn or less. It didn't seem like much but it was a drastic change, resulting in a lot of different things happening.

To many who don't play golf it would be considered an infinitesimal change. But it was a fault that had cost me many thousands of dollars over the past two plus years. During my first three years on tour I had managed to rank high in Performance Averages and money won. Then my problems set in, and until I won the Phoenix Open in 1959 I had not won an event since the Tournament of Champions in 1957. That's a long spell with no wins.

After Paul made the minor adjustment in my grip he stepped up to the tee. He imitated how I used to swing and then how I was swinging now. As I carefully compared every phase of the two swings, I noticed a big difference. My current arc included a definite "loop" at the start of the downswing where I dropped the club down to a flatter swing plane.

Runyan, whom many consider the finest professor for a professional in the game, seemed to hit at the heart of my problems. Because of my incorrect right-hand grip I was falling into a number of faults. He did nothing to my left-hand position on the grip.

Once I had corrected the grip, Paul then paid close attention to my waggle, which is an important part of the swing because it is a preview of the action of the actual swing. With my wrong grip the heel of the clubhead waggled more than the toe. This, in effect, kept the clubface closed on the waggle and necessarily during the swing itself. This is not a natural action and prior to 1957 I did not do it.

Runyan, a brilliant and introspective man, was one of the most able diagnosticians of what is wrong with a golf swing that there has ever been.

First he explained what the incorrect grip was doing. When I swung the club back with the bad grip the clubface would be shut at the top. Then as I came down if I released the club-head I would hit a big hook, and if I didn't release, the result was a push. The loop was created by an instinctive effort to guard against hooking.

With the altered right-hand grip and the proper waggle, I started making practice shots under Paul's ever-watchful eye. At first most of them were to the right because the clubface was more open at the top of the swing, but Paul assured me that I could hit as hard as I wanted to and soon the shots would straighten out.

Almost instantly I could feel that I was hitting the ball more solidly than I had for two years. Believe me, it was a great feeling. The end result was a more upright swing and a feeling that I could get the ball onto the center of the clubface every time. My iron shots began flying high and they had good back-spin on them. Even the long irons stopped well on the greens.

All told, in that initial session we probably spent no more than an hour. But that hour in November of 1958 was the best investment in time that I have ever made. After that Paul would check me occasionally while giving lessons to others on the practice tee, usually when he would note a slight fault that he felt I should correct.

We talked a lot during that winter—through the months of November and December—before I resumed the tour with the Los Angeles Open on January 2, 1959. We did more talking than we did work because all my tinkering and all the advice I received from my fellow pros who were all trying their best to help just seemed to botch things up. To say I was confused was putting it mildly. But by the time I got in the car and headed north for the Rancho Golf Course on Pico Boulevard and the Los Angeles Open, my mind and my golf seemed to be on the right track.

The first round felt pretty good with a 70, but then . . . disaster—74–73–74 and a 291 total. My check for $161.43 wouldn't pay my board and room let alone anything else. Then I came back home for a day or two, talked to Paul some more, hit a lot more balls off the practice tee and headed for the Tijuana Open across the border at the Tijuana Country Club.

It wasn't very good either. Another 33rd, one stroke behind the final pay spot; but even if I had been at 283 I would have earned only $55. Even in low-cost Tijuana that wouldn't pay the bills.

There were five days between the close at Tijuana and the first round in the Bing Crosby National Pro-Am up on the Monterey Peninsula's three courses—Cypress Point, Monterey, and Pebble Beach.

I'd never really had a true golf lesson in my life—for which I or my parents had paid a pro—but right then I sure wished I had. So I then went back to La Jolla and the practice tee rather than going directly to Bing's Clambake. I needed some more of Paul Runyan's choice bits of advice, but, most important, I had to get in the swing groove or 1959 was going to pale those horrible years of 1957 and 1958. To say it simply . . . I was rotten.

Paul assured me things were right, that I just had to be confident and let it all hang out when I swung. Monday and Tuesday of that week I hit balls by the hundreds, played a round or two with Paul and finally left Tuesday night for Pebble Beach and hopefully a decent practice round on Wednesday.

Runyan certainly has been one of my biggest boosters. I'll always remember a remark he made at Augusta during the 1956 Masters to one of the writers: "They say the three best long iron players of all time were Hogan, Snead, and Nelson. Well, I'll take Littler over any of 'em. He's simply wonderful with long irons."

I reminded him about statements like that while we were

trying to untangle my game during that '58–59 winter, especially the days before heading north for the Crosby. I was terribly dissatisfied with everything. If I hadn't been such a determined cuss I might have chucked the whole thing and gone on to restoring cars.

And after my first round in the Crosby I was just about ready to begin beating on fenders. I shot a 73 and thought to myself that I was pretty well along to shooting myself right out of contention. But then things seemed to fall in place. My drives were better, my irons crisp and my putter seemed to know where the cup was. I added a 67–70 going into the final round, and found myself with a pretty good chance to make a run for the top shot. There was $4,000 to the winner, and while it wasn't ten grand like at Las Vegas, it was mighty nice to contemplate.

There has been a great deal of confusion about that final round at Crosby in 1959. The story goes that I was leading the tournament going into 18 and plunked the ball in the Pacific. The real truth is that I was a stroke back of Art Wall, Jr., who had led me by about six or seven strokes after nine, and I did hit my second shot into the drink.

It was a disastrous hook with my second wood, and it may or may not have cost me the tournament since Art was up by one going to the hole. All I can say is that this was the only wide hook I hit during all the tournament. Since the changes Paul made in my grip and swing were small, I must have forgotten his advice for the moment.

As it turned out, Wall made a six on 18 and if I hadn't hit that big pond I might have had a shot at a win or a tie. But then again, he might not have taken a six if I had stayed on the course.

Anyway, he won by two at 279, but that $2,150 second-money check I took home in a tie with Jimmy Demaret was one of the brightest and biggest in some time. I felt that I had whipped my problems and 1959 was going to be a glorious year.

It wasn't long until such dreams became reality. Going down to Phoenix the first week in February for the Phoenix

Open Invitational at the Arizona Country Club, I shot 67–63–67–71—268 to beat Art Wall, Jr., by a shot and win $2,400. The next week in the Tucson Open Invitational at El Rio Country Club it was 65–67–68–66—266 and my first back-to-back win, with a top prize of $2,000. Seven of my eight rounds in those two weeks were in the 60s, giving me up to that point on the winter tour nine rounds in the 60s and three in the 70s.

Mr. Runyan's diagnostic work was accurate. I was convinced that at least I had my swing problems under control. Now it was a day-to-day thing to keep my concentration in line and maintain the swing style Paul Runyan had so carefully rebuilt.

16

We had acquired our first home just before Christmas in 1955. It was a little three-bedroom tract house of maybe 1500 square feet up on the Claremont mesa, a kind of butte overlooking Mission Bay. My dad knew the developers and, because of that, we were able to make a few changes, such as enlarging the master bedroom. Shirley was able to pick out the light fixtures and some other little decorator items to give it a personal touch.

We paid about $20,000 for it, in those days a lot of money for two young kids a little over a year on the golf tour. But it was a terrific little house, and we enjoyed it. Since we expected other children to come along we needed a third bedroom. Suzy didn't arrive until almost two years later but we were ready for her.

As both of the children began to grow up, we were convinced we needed more space, both inside and out. In the meantime we had taken an option on a lot in Muirland, about a block and a half from my dad's home on La Jolla Rancho Road. We'd fallen in love with the lot when we'd drive by going to see him. Dad's situation with the Hazard Company had made it possible to put a hold or a reservation on it for us since we liked it so well; so it had been ours for a long time although we didn't actually pay for it until December or so of 1958.

Knowing it was going to be ours, Shirley had been clipping house plans, decorator ideas, and floor plans of almost everything she liked. So one day in December we just decided to build, bought the lot, and sat down with the architect-builder, Ralph Crane, to tell him what we wanted. Within thirty days we had approved his floor plan and drawings. Then in January we took off, leaving everything in his hands.

When we took a break on the tour and came home in April the house was well along, framed in, and we could see what it was going to be like. I was amazed. It just about matched what Shirley and I had dreamed about.

About the first week in August we came home again hoping it would be done but it wasn't. We went into a motel for a few days and finally we just moved in with the builders. It seemed to take so long for the finish work—the cabinets, the paneling, the detail work. I was climbing the walls and finally I just joined in to get things done.

But we really love it. The lot is great, about an acre in size—approximately 160 feet across the front of the street and 300 feet deep. Of course, most of that 300 feet is in a gully back behind the garage. The house is pretty good-sized—about 3,500 square feet, with four bedrooms, a family room, a formal dining room, living room, kitchen, laundry, a little office cubicle where we both work, and three and a half baths.

After winning the $35,000 Miller Open in Milwaukee on the last day of August in 1959, I remember telling the press that the $5,300 first-prize money was going to help furnish our new home. (That was the first time a pro had won five tournaments in a year since Cary Middlecoff did it in 1955.) Some of the furniture in our living room and family room today we can credit to that Miller Open. It still looks pretty good to me. So far Shirley hasn't talked about changing it and that's good too.

We believed we had given enough thought over the years to what we wanted in a house. The one thing I wanted, and probably the only thing I personally planned, was the garage.

I wanted an oversized three-car garage, and it turned out to be a dandy.

There was only one thing wrong. I got to the point where I had too many cars, and Shirley kept talking about a swimming pool. After shuffling cars back and forth on the garage apron for too many years, we finally decided to add on another garage and at the same time to build a swimming pool and a cabaña for the pool.

I guess I kind of bribed Shirley. I told her I'd go for the pool if she would go for the garage. Little did we know what we were getting into. We built it all together and it turned into quite a fiasco.

Everything seemed to snowball, cost-wise. We had to have an architect-engineer because part of the garage had to be built on fill. We ended up putting seven pillars of concrete four feet in diameter down somewhere near China. They were about thirty-four feet deep, and the concrete trucks never seemed to stop. The ultimate bill was a fortune.

One of the concrete pillars was my doing. I wanted a hydraulic lift in the new garage so I could easily hoist the cars up to work on them. Then one of the little things we forgot about when we figured the garage height was the fact the lift would take a car up quite a ways. We had to revise the plans to allow more height for some of the old cars that were taller than current models.

That meant we had to have a different garage door so the architect (who, incidentally, did a super job and was very helpful) worked out this door that breaks in sections and rolls up into the roof. But it all got out of hand, costing about three times as much as we'd planned to spend. The whole thing—pool, garage, lift, cabaña, a little new siding on the house, and a whole new paint job—ran out almost to the dollar what it had cost to build the entire original house in 1959.

It was what we wanted. Now we can garage six cars but the same old condition exists. I've got more cars than garage space and we're back to shuffling cars. That's a little tougher than shuffling cards.

I've strolled down the gully behind the new garage a time

or two thinking about making a big circle drive around the house and adding on some more garage space. Every time I sell one of my antique cars I regret it. They appreciate so fast that they are a good investment. I would like to hold onto them but they must be garaged, and I've never had the courage to broach Shirley with another addition.

Besides, much as we hate to admit it, it won't be too long before there will just be two of us rattling around in this big house. Curt's only around during vacations and in the summer. And we miss him. I especially miss him out in the garage. He's a pretty good mechanic; loves to do the same things I do. Since he's been doing them with me for years we think alike.

He also keeps the house alive with his music. He has taught himself to play the piano and banjo, and he's good on ragtime music, which I really love. I offered to arrange for him to take lessons but he wanted no part of them.

It all began six or seven years ago when I bought Shirley a piano. She had played and was quite good but never seemed to sit down and use it. Curt came in one day and started beating on it, and away he went. In no time at all he was playing up a storm. Every time he plays now I think he is better.

He hopes to become a medical doctor, and in today's competition that's mighty rough. Just getting into medical school takes a lot of doing. However, Curt is a dedicated young man and I know he'll make it.

The past two summers he has stayed home to work rather than go with us on tour. In the summer of 1974 he worked on a research project at Scripps Clinic here in La Jolla.

The year before both Curt and Suzy went with us to the British Open. Probably the highlight of the trip as far as they were concerned—and we sure enjoyed it also—was going to Wimbledon for the tennis championships.

Both Curt and Suzy prefer tennis to golf. Neither one can see the time it takes to play a round of golf nor the practice time it requires to increase your proficiency. I understand that, and I am just happy that they are active, good kids finding their place in life.

Suzy is now at Pepperdine University, the Malibu campus.

It's sad to realize that once they start college they're not going to be around home much. Now we understand how our parents felt when we left, but when you're young you don't think that way. I guess every young person feels his parents are too possessive.

Maybe Curt's love for cars will keep bringing him back. That's one thing we have in common.

About four or five years ago I followed through on a chance to buy a 1955 T-bird. It's Curt's car now although he doesn't take it up to Stanford. He leaves it here for safekeeping and around school drives an old Mustang he bought. We have rebuilt his Bird from top to bottom. The engine has all been gone through, the transmission, brakes, everything. It has a stick shift, it purrs like a kitten, and with its yellow paint job a lot of people stop and want to buy it. I drive it once a week when I'm home and he's at school, just to keep it sharp.

One of the most relaxing things I've found is tinkering with cars. I'm fairly mechanically inclined but not a great auto mechanic. I can do minor mechanical work such as tune-ups and so forth but I can't rebore an engine or attempt any major work. Those things I have to hire done.

Body work is another story. I can refinish the bodies, sand, paint, and do almost any kind of restoration.

Out in the garage I can forget all my troubles. All the three-putt greens, the shots I shanked and the shots that didn't turn out right. Usually I come home from the tour to relax a bit and get my game back in shape to go out again. Only trouble is that I may get so wound up fixing a car that I don't practice. It can become a bad deal from the viewpoint of competitive golf.

So, for the next few years, I'm going to concentrate more on golf and not put so much work on cars. With both of the kids gone to college Shirley can go out with me more. I want to give the tour a real shake and just see how well I can do. I'm still going to come home every once in a while but instead of every two weeks maybe it will be a month. You can be sure I'll still be banging a few fenders out, sanding down some hoods and painting doors, but there will also be considerable practice time at La Jolla.

I don't smoke and don't drink, but I assume one becomes addicted to both just as I have to cars. I can't tell you just when that took place but I was mighty young. Even as a youngster I always stopped to watch an old car go by. My interest in antique cars has developed since I became a professional golfer and had the wherewithal to invest in classic chassis. Now I truly appreciate them because I know the hundreds of hours that have gone into restoring them, not to mention the dollars.

Exactly how many cars I have owned over the years is impossible to say. Any figure I'd give would be a guess, but it's probably close to a hundred.

Some of the more interesting ones I acquired and restored since my dad helped me get that first 1933 Ford two-door sedan bring back fond memories.

There were the 1952 Javelin Jupiter; a couple of large Cadillacs; four different single-seater T-Birds; three XKE Jags; the 1924 Rolls roadster; 1929 Rolls Phaeton;1937 Rolls Wraith; 1952 Rolls Silver Dawn; and those I now have—the 1956 Rolls Silver Cloud, the 1929 Rolls Formal Town Sedan, and the 1968 maroon Silver Shadow convertible.

As I write this, I have just closed a deal with my car-buff friend in Monterey, Dave Taylor, for another Rolls—a 1925 Silver Ghost Piccadilly Roadster. It's identical to the '24 I always regretted selling. It will create that same old problem— where to store it while I complete the exterior and interior restoration.

For a while in my car-collecting career, I was on a Ford kick. I had a 1935 Ford convertible; then a 1928 Model A four-door; a 1931 Model A two-door sedan; a 1930 Model A pickup truck; a 1930 Model A roadster; a 1914 and a 1915 Model T roadster and a 1920 Model T Phaeton touring sedan.

I was in love with every one of them. I sure wish I had some of them now—especially the '24 and '29 Rolls— but space just made storage too difficult.

Over the years some of my friends have often kidded me about my car collection. "Gene," one of them told me once, "you're going to have to get a used car dealer's license if you keep selling cars." (I think if you sell more than six or seven cars a year you have to have a dealer's license.)

My friend Dave Taylor told me about a fellow who was part-owner of British Motors. This fellow had a 1929 Rolls Royce Phaeton that he had to sell for one reason or another. Dave called me one day and wanted to know if I wanted to buy it.

"Gee, Dave," I said, "that sounds like a great idea. How much do they want for it?"

I think he told me $8,000, and I said yes, although I had never seen it; just agreed to buy it on Dave's say-so over the telephone. In no time at all, the owner's wife and another lady had brought it down to La Jolla to me. I'd only partially restored it when one day Dave Taylor wanted to buy it back. He totally restored it and won best-of-show at the Pebble Beach *Concours d'élégance.*

Not long after that I bought it back from Dave, but this time it cost me $15,000. An Ascot Phaeton model, a four-door with a convertible top, it was a beauty and I kept it for a long time, until one day Dick Martin asked me if I would auction it off at the Comedians' Golf Classic. It brought $21,000 at the auction with part of the proceeds going to charity. Except for what that money accomplished, I wish I had kept it. It was truly a beautiful car.

That Rolls hooked me on restoring antique cars.

Next I bought a 1924 Rolls Royce roadster. After it was all fixed up and in top shape, I took Shirley, Curt, and Suzy up to spend the day at Disneyland. I've never had so many people honk at me or come up to me in any car as that one.

Over the years I've had nine Rollses. They are really super machines, so perfect for their day, way overbuilt. Someone in England told me that during World War I they took the bodies off Rolls Royces, slipped a tank chassis over them, and used them in combat. Then they brought them back and slipped the bodies back on.

I have four left. One is a 1929 Rolls Formal Town Sedan, a chauffeur-driven job. The way I bought it makes a funny story. I was restoring a 1952 Rolls and had pulled the engine out and tossed it in the back of a pickup we borrowed to take it up north for rebuilding. That was the fall of Curt's first year at Stanford, and we were going to do a lot of things in one trip: get Curt to Palo Alto, drop the engine off at San Lorenzo to be rebuilt, and return home. When we drove into the garage in San Lorenzo the first thing I noticed was this Town Sedan sitting out in front.

"Is that car for sale?" I asked before I even unloaded the '52 engine.

"Yeah, I think so," said the mechanic. The next thing I knew we had the owner on the phone, and minutes after we unloaded the engine to be rebuilt I drove off with the Town Sedan toward Stanford. I think they had set me up for that buy.

That's a trip Shirley and I will never forget. She drove the pickup back while I drove the Rolls. It had a radiator problem —the only thing mechanically wrong with it—so every five miles we had to stop and tank up with water. It took us about sixteen hours to get home. We didn't hit the driveway until about 4:00 A.M., almost daylight.

That was in September of 1973 and we still haven't begun restoring it. It doesn't need any mechanical work to speak of. The body has no dings in it but it is so big it will take months to strip it down, prime it, and get ready for the color coat.

I guess that's the problem. Shirley and I have talked a lot about the color, consulted the Rolls Royce antique guide, but haven't been able to decide. We are leaning towards making the body cranberry red with a black top and pearl gray mohair upholstery. The original crystal vases are in the rear seats and we've pictured them with yellow-beaded roses in them.

The biggest problem with antiques like the Rolls is that you are limited as to where you can drive them. They'll go anywhere but you've got to be very careful where you park them. You need a secure place because for some strange reason people want to vandalize them. People don't always give a fine car the consideration it should have.

We had a 1958 righthand-drive Rolls Royce sedan—the one I restored right after my surgery. "Restored" is not quite the right word because a 1958 is not an antique, but I put a lot of work into it. Shirley drove that a lot and so did I if we were all going out together. It was really a machine. It was big, and looked even larger because it was all white. But I sold it and bought a 1956 sable and sand Silver Cloud. It's also a four-door lefthand drive and a beauty.

I guess I'm a little different from a lot of the antique collectors. I'm not really interested in keeping the cars all polished up for shows. I want to restore their engines to where they run perfectly and then drive them. I don't want to be trucking them weekend after weekend to some show. I've always made it a practice to drive every car I have ever owned, alternating them to keep them all in top running shape.

One of my vices, at home or away, is reading the car want-ads. Reading the *San Diego Union* one day, I came across this 1965 Jaguar XKE for sale. The owner, a high-diver at Sea World, was moving to Florida and wanted to sell the car. When I bought it, that started me on a six-month restoration project, which I've almost finished now. Taking the engine out to get it worked over was a bear. With the hood off you have at least half the car exposed, but getting it all apart is something. It comes down to trial and error—mostly error. Getting the windows back in was something else. It takes patience just as it does to get the headlamp lenses in properly.

Once you get it all back together, however, you have something that is beautiful. And unlike the case with some other hobbies, restored cars increase in value with every passing day.

Because of my cars I had to buy a commercial sewing machine. I've had this big Singer for five or six years, but I had to learn the hard way how to make it work. Singer doesn't put out a manual for commercial machines.

I just about went crazy trying to make a vinyl cover for the gearbox on the Jaguar. I finally had to enlist Shirley's aid and her machine. Finally we made a cover that has a pretty snug fit. I didn't find out until afterwards that you have to buy a special foot with a plastic bottom for the Singer so it will glide over the vinyl without hanging up the stitch.

I bought the machine to redo the leather upholstery on the 1924 Rolls roadster. I bought ten hides of leather and started in.

I quickly realized I was way over my head and took the whole thing to a professional to do.

Right now we have the 1956 Rolls that I call Shirley's car; the 1929 Rolls Town Sedan; the Jag; the black 1965 Porsche; Curt's yellow T-Bird; the 1925 Silver Ghost Piccadilly Roadster; the 1968 Silver Shadow convertible; and Suzy's VW station wagon.

The Jensen was like the Facel Vegas I owned and wish I had kept. Both were Chrysler-powered, and the old hemi engine in the Vega was great. But each time another car that I wanted came along and I was fresh out of garage space, so something had to give.

Time is the big factor in restorations but garage space isn't far behind. Keeping every car I've ever restored is something I sometimes think I'd like to have done. But that would be even worse than thinking about building in the gully. We'd have to have a warehouse.

17 O▬O▬O▬O▬O▬O▬O▬O▬

It took me nearly a month to break into the money in 1961 and that was a 40th-place finish in the Lucky International Open at Harding Park Course in San Francisco. That was the last week in January and I won the munificent total of $116.

Then I went until the first week in April and the Masters at Augusta National before winning another dime. My finish in a tie for 12th with Stan Leonard, Sam Snead, and Bob Rosburg at 289 won me $1,300.

The very next week in the Greater Greensboro Open Invitational I shot another 289 and ended up in a tie with Bert Weaver and Doug Sanders for 10th and $800.

By now I had lost my magic in the Tournament of Champions, but my scores seemed to be permanently stuck on 289 as I finished there again in a tie for 13th with Ken Venturi and Billy Maxwell for $1,500.

I finally got out of the 289 rut the next week in the Colonial National Invitational in Fort Worth, shooting a 284 to tie Don Whitt, whom I'd been with in the Navy in San Diego, for fourth place and $1,900.

1961 seemed to be my year for repetitive scores. In the "500" Festival Open Tournament during the Indianapolis race week at Speedway Golf Club I shot another 284 to tie Bill Collins and Ken Still for 19th and $850.

Then in the Memphis Open, two weeks before the U.S. Open, my game suddenly came together. I shot rounds of 66–69–69–69 —273 for fifth place behind Cary Middlecoff's 266. With $1,400 coming from my tie with Buddy Sullivan and Lionel Herbert I felt real comfortable as we went on to Detroit to practice the week before the Open began at Oakland Hills Country Club in suburban Birmingham.

The Open had been a difficult tournament for me over the years after I came so close that first season in 1954 by finishing second to Ed Furgol. My best after that was fourth in 1958, and my total winnings in six years came to $3,280, just a shade below the $3,600 I got for second in 1954.

After checking the family into the nearby motel in Detroit, I drove out to Oakland Hills to practice. Back in those days I played a lot of practice rounds with Ted Kroll. We always tried to help one another straighten out some minor flaw or error. During a practice round with Ted, either the first or second day, after a few holes he told me: "Gene, I think you're swinging too flat. If I were you I'd try to swing a little more upright."

I tried it for the rest of that round and a couple more, and it felt pretty good. The adjustment was really minor. When you're too flat you are swinging below the intended swing plane, which varies for each individual according to height.

I did not get off to a roaring start in the 61st National Open but no one else really did either. Bob Brue was the first-round leader at 69, and my 73 was not so far back that I was worried. I was never big on the leaderboard during the entire tournament. In fact, going into the second 18 holes of the final day 36-hole affair I was tied for seventh, three strokes off the pace set by Doug Sanders—the only one in the field of fifty-seven at even par.

Back of Doug a stroke were Bob Goalby, Mike Souchak (a couple of strong, long-hitting former college football stars), and Jacky Cupit. Back two to four strokes were Doug Ford,

Gardner Dickinson, Eric Monti, Bob Rosburg, Allen Geiberger, Brue, Dow Finsterwald, Jack Nicklaus and me.

There were many in the gallery and fewer in the press tent who gave any of us much chance of catching Sanders, especially as he seemed to hold things together well in the early part of the afternoon round.

They estimated the gallery that day at 20,000 but few were watching Gardner Dickinson and me. In fact, Jack Murphy, who had come east from San Diego to cover the open for the *Union,* counted seven people in our gallery on the third hole. It might have been ten but Shirley, Curt and Suzy were back in the hotel in Detroit. It was pretty hard for youngsters—especially Suzy, who was just past three—to walk a full eighteen holes.

By the 11th there may have been a hundred. It was here I began to move, scoring birdies on 11 and 13 while Sanders—I learned later—was going over par on 9, 10, and 12. All of a sudden I was three shots in front of Sanders and two ahead of Goalby.

I was playing for the second round in a row with Gardner Dickinson, who by 15 had shot himself out of the tournament and was trying to keep me just a little loose as we played out the round.

"I'll sell you that shot," Gardner told me after hitting a fine drive on 16. But mine was even better so I didn't take him up on the offer.

It wasn't until we were walking up to the 16th green that I myself realized I was ahead of Sanders and Goalby. There was a leaderboard just off the green that showed me in front, but Doug was about two holes behind us.

I two-putted from a somewhat treacherous spot on 17. Things were getting pretty tense. I figured that if I parred the last hole I would at least tie, and maybe win, but a bogey would definitely hurt.

The 18th hole at Oakland Hills is very difficult, with a very narrow fairway and a long, demanding second shot after a real good drive. I probably had a two-iron shot but decided to try a fade with a four-wood because I was playing that shot well, and besides, I had just hit the same shot on 17. Unfortunately, the shot did not fade. I dropped into a deep sand trap that closed off a good part of the large, undulating green now rimmed with most of the 20,000 spectators.

I came out of the trap all right, but I had wanted to get the ball to the back of the green near the hole. I exploded with a lot of sand, however, to guard against a possible sculled shot. (Sometimes when you have a long trap shot you tend to swing too close to the ball in an effort to reach the hole.) I left myself about seventeen feet short of the pin. My first putt was weak—perhaps the pressure was getting to me as Sanders had cut my lead to a shot—and I was left with about a two-footer.

I've never been one to study a putt for a great length of time, but I do recall looking it over quite carefully before stepping up and knocking it in the hole.

I was the leader, but Sanders still had 17 and 18 to play and was behind by only one stroke. A birdie on either would tie me and force a playoff. His fourteen-foot putt on 17 for a two ran around the lip and out.

By now I was in the clubhouse watching things on TV. Doug drove poorly on 18, catching the rough off to the right, but the large gallery had trampled the grass down so much he had a fairly good lie. His two-iron faded around a clump of small evergreens and stopped about eight to ten feet short of the green.

Using about a nine-iron for the chip, Doug made a magnificent shot that seemed destined for the hole, but at the brink of the cup it bent left a bit and missed—by no more than an inch. The U.S. Open was mine.

"Was that last putt a straight-in putt?" someone asked me in the press conference after the presentation of the $14,000 first-prize check.

"It was straight in," I said; "at least I thought it was. I couldn't see the hole."

As I was sitting watching Doug's final chip I thought back seven years before when I was in a similar situation at Baltusrol, needing a putt of about eight feet to tie Ed Furgol my first year as a pro, and missed. I knew how Doug felt. Just like I did. All drained out. When they don't drop in a tight situation like that with so much riding on the putt, as you miss you feel as if all the blood has run down your legs and out your spikes.

With the win in the Open I joined some select company. Only a few have won the U.S. Amateur and the U.S. Open during their careers, one of the writers pointed out. A lot of the names were just legends. Only Arnold Palmer was from my era. Francis Ouimet, Chick Evans, Bobby Jones, Lawson Little, and Johnny Goodman were names I dreamed about when I was a kid.

Now here I was, surrounded by all the writers, photographers, sportscasters, and TV cameras, trying to do one of the things I find most difficult. My mind was wandering off. I wondered if Shirley, Curt and Suzy had seen the close of the tournament on TV.

"Did the rough bother you?" a writer asked, bringing me back to the reality of the moment.

"No, I don't think so. I stayed out of most of it."

"Did you ever think of giving up the tour, Gene?"

"I felt like it often but my wife wouldn't let me. A few years ago I was playing so poorly I had about decided to give up professional golf.

"And I probably would have too, but Shirley kept me going. She has a super attitude and she said I should stick with it, that things were certain to get better. I only regret that she wasn't here to see me win. She was baby-sitting with our children in our hotel."

"When did you know what you had to do?" another asked.

"I knew at 16. I just wanted to shoot for pars the rest of the way. The last hole is the toughest on the course. I don't mind admitting I was scared of it."

"Did you ever think you might lose?" asked someone in the back.

"I wasn't ever in a position to lose it. Except maybe on the last hole, I guess."

"What did you figure it would take to win?"

"I predicted that a 284 or a 285 would win. I'm certainly glad I didn't shoot either."

I won with a 281, a shot ahead of Goalby and Sanders.

Someone asked me about the fact that I had only three three-putt greens out of the seventy-two holes.

"Putting is a tremendous part of this game," I said, "as everybody knows. In the past year I started to putt a little better. In that time I tried a thousand strokes and stances.

"I used a half dozen different putters in the last year," I admitted. "I even made one myself. Finally I went back to the old type of putter I had used as an amateur."

Somewhere, somehow, out of that long interview the story developed that I had used a $1.50 putter I had picked up one time from a miniature golf course.

I did buy a putter from a miniature golf course. I think it was in Milwaukee. Fred Hawkins and I used to travel together when our children were real young. One time we took them to a miniature putt-putt course. They had a rack of putters on a counter and I grabbed one.

It looked pretty good to me, and after we had played I bought it from the manager for a dollar and a half or so. I know it was not much more than a dollar. I took it home to my shop and put my own shaft in it.

I did use it in the Lucky International—one of the early tournaments—but in 1962, not 1961. It's ironic that a story about that win got it mixed up too. The writer said that I had got into the rough on one hole about eighty yards from the pin, and since there was no room to swing a club righthanded, which was true, I pulled out the $1.50 putter, which was also true. And I did hit the ball up on the green lefthanded, which was quite a shot, but not into the cup as the writer claimed.

I don't really know how things such as that get all twisted around and confused with other shots and other tournaments, but they do.

Still another example of mixed-up reporting happened when I took a course called PACE (Personal and Company Effectiveness). It's run by Jim Newman in Los Angeles and is basically a motivational, power-of-positive-thinking course. Shirley took it with me and later on Curt went. It was very beneficial to me personally and I believed helped my confidence in golf.

Somehow the facts got twisted around to where a news story said I was paying a psychologist $700 a month to improve my self-confidence.

It's true that I'm not happy when I'm not playing well. (Show me a professional who is.) Since I'm somewhat of a perfectionist, it is only natural that it bothers me when I don't play up to my capabilities. But I don't carry my woes off the course and home with me. I try to leave those problems at the course so when I get home I can enjoy being with my family.

I wouldn't trade fifty major championships for the life style we have lived over these years. I've never put anything above my family and I never will. Championships are nice to win, the money—especially now—is great, and when you can make that much doing something you really enjoy, that's quite a life.

My friend Gary Player, whom I truly admire as a man and a golfer, told the press that I was "the best husband on the tour." Now that is truly appreciated, especially coming from such a wonderful family man as Gary, who is so dedicated himself.

When you read and hear things like that it makes you warm inside. It makes you love your fellowman and realize that you need the help of the Lord to get by day to day. Not on the golf course, not in your endeavor but in your total life. Sunday service is important to me at Christ Lutheran Church down the hill from my house in Pacific Beach. I hate to miss it. But when I'm out on tour, since we play every Sunday, it is next to impossible to go.

We've got some very devout people in professional golf. I don't think there is any question that the confidence gained from deep religious convictions is beneficial. I think it can improve your golf score, your sales record, and help you live a happier family life. Faith can do wonders.

The world is full of good people in all walks of life. I met hundreds of them before, during, and after my surgery. People that counted and people who were just part of our life. Basically, they were all good. Every once in a while I'll go back and read some of the letters that came to me at Mercy Hospital and home.

One of them I deeply cherish. It reads:

Dear Gene:

I was terribly sorry to have read about your illness, especially since you have always been such a perfect gentleman and a credit to all mankind.

If it is any consolation you must know that no one goes through life with perfect health. Those who have faith, determination and will, overcome these bad interludes in their lives.

If I know you—and I think I do—you possess these qualities and will soon be back at your work.

May I commend you for being the kind of a person that you are and wish you well with a speedy recovery.

Sincerely,

Ben

Those were Ben Hogan's words. When one thinks of the comeback he made from his horrible auto accident to dominate world golf as few men have ever done, his words are truly appreciated. Ben Hogan was the master of his era, and when I reread his words I feel awfully humble.

Ben gathered golf championships at a remarkable pace in the days when $10,000 total prize was a big tournament. I thought about that when I won the U.S. Open at Oakland Hills in 1961. Ben finished twelfth and won $900 but he had won the Open in 1948, 1950, 1951, and 1953. A remarkable record by a remarkable man.

When I got home from the 1961 Open there was a mound of mail from friends, former golfing partners, people I have met over the years on tour. Each one had wonderful things to say.

One came from a master of self-control and assurance, and a man I have always admired.

July 5, 1961

Dear Gene:

A little late, perhaps, but I've been fishing and wanted to add my congratulations to the thousands of others you must have received for your great win in the National Open Championship.

I can't think of a more popular victor than you and, without question, you must have played flawlessly to tame that course, which according to all reports was very tough indeed.

I hope this presages a great year for you and more greater years to come.

As ever,

Bing Crosby.

Nice words from a nice man who puts on one of the great golf tournaments in the world.

Gene Littler works on golf grip at La Jolla Country Club under watchful eye of Paul Runyan, then head professional. It was Runyan who revised Littler's grip and turned his career around after nearly two-year slump. (UPI Telephoto)

Runner-up George Knudson (left) examines bargain putter used by Gene Littler to win San Francisco International golf championship. (Wide World Photo)

Gene tries for birdie on 9th green in final round of 1961 U.S. Open at Birmingham, Michigan. Though he missed this shot, he went on to win the prestigious tournament. (Wide World Photo)

Three generations of Littlers. Grandson, Curt; father, Fred; son, Gene at Borrego Springs Country Club near San Diego.

Shirley and Gene during Ryder Cup matches with Great Britain at Royal Brookdale Course outside London. (Bill Mark photo)

A rare occasion: Gene in formal attire, ready to enter residence of Lord Mayor of London during Ryder Cup affair in England. (Bill Mark photo)

Gene surrounds World Series of Golf trophy after win in September 1966. Tied with Allen Geiberger and Jack Nicklaus at the end of 36 holes, Gene birdied 37 to take the $50,000 prize, the largest check he had earned to that date.

Champions have their share of trouble shots. Gene made short chip from here to be in position for birdie during first round of 1965 Thunderbird Classic and eventually a sizzling 66 for the day. (Wide World Photo)

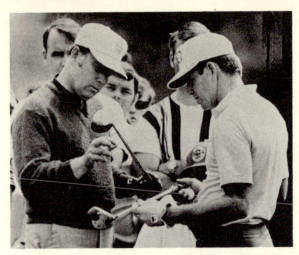

Left: At 1970 Masters, Billy Casper (left) and Gene tied at 279 after regulation 72 holes. Here they compare drivers as they wait to begin playoff, which Casper won. Below: Gene celebrates birdie on 15th during final round. (Wide World Photo)

Gene executes long drive at Colonial National Invitational tournament in
Fort Worth, Texas. At left with hands on hips, Mike Souchak waits for
Arnold Palmer (behind Gene) to tee off next. Scoreboard shows Littler 2
under, Palmer 3 under, and Souchak 3 over. Gene won this tournament
in 1971 with a 283.

Jack Nicklaus
reaches between
Harry Bannerman
and Peter Townsend
of the British Ryder
Cup team to shake
hands with Gene
Littler, his partner in
a Friday morning
match which they
won for the U.S.
team in September
1971 at Old Warson
Country Club
near St. Louis.
(Wide World Photo)

Gene, Curt, Suzy
and friend Lisa
Rights wash
Thunderbird restored
by Gene and Curt.

Curt Littler
poses with
1924 Rolls
Royce Silver
Ghost coupe
restored by
Gene to mint
condition
and later
regretfully
sold.

Gene with
Suzy and
Curt in
September
1972 with
1929 Rolls
Royce Town
Sedan
purchased
when they
took Curt to
Stanford for
his first year
of school.

Dave Taylor, Gene's longtime friend who got him hooked on antique car restoration, checks out 1929 Rolls Royce Phaeton Sedan in driveway of Taylor home.

Right: Christmas 1973, Curt, Shirley, and Suzy with 1958 Rolls Silver Cloud I that Gene restored during his recuperation from cancer surgery. Below: Curt and Suzy in November 1969 with fully restored 1929 Rolls Royce Phaeton Sedan.

Curt, Suzy, and Shirley Littler are part of gallery for Swing at Cancer benefit at Del Pasos Country Club in Sacramento, California, in 1974.

Below: Gene Littler warms up before teeing off in the Swing at Cancer Pro-Amateur tournament. Watching are singer John Raitt and California Supreme Court Justice Hugh Evans.

Defending champion Lee Trevino (right) with Gene Littler during third round play in St. Louis Children's Hospital Classic in July 1973. Gene's win in this tournament was his first following cancer surgery. (Wide World Photo)

Gene and Bing Crosby chat during lull in tournament play at Bing Crosby National. Gene was 1975 winner. (San Diego Union-Tribune photo by Dan Tichonchuk)

Gene plays in the rain in Tokyo in 1974 to win the
Pacific Masters championship and $65,000.

18

As the holidays of 1961 came to a close I was looking forward to the Crosby, as most of the golfers and those in the golf world call it. That tournament traditionally used to start off the tour each year in January, and it is one of my favorite affairs.

My second-place finish in total earnings in 1961 had me feeling pretty good about how I was doing as a pro on tour. That indicator is also important when it comes to paying the bills.

But 1962 didn't come ringing in with any great chime of silver dollars as I finished 12th, 15th, and 18th in three turn-of-the-year events—the Los Angeles Open, the San Diego Open, and the Crosby. I never broke 70 in Bing's affair and I wondered if there was going to be "another great year."

The week after the Crosby, however, things fell into place and I won the Lucky International Open with that $1.50 putter and picked up $9,000.

That was a year of close finishes but not quite championships, although the first week in June I won the Thunderbird Classic Invitational, the forerunner of the Westchester Classic, at the Upper Montclair Country Club in New Jersey. It was a fat purse—$25,000—and I beat Jack Nicklaus, playing his first year on the tour, by two shots.

141

It was the week before I had to defend my U.S. Open title, and I had to shoot a 67 to beat Nicklaus out of $15,000—the difference between first and second money.

I started the final round a stroke back of Jack and Dow Finsterwald, who were tied at 207. I remember catching them with a birdie on the first hole. Jack and I were in the same threesome so we were head and head all the way around the final round.

At one point I had a five-shot lead over Jack, but when you're playing side by side with him you feel it, and during the late holes I became a little wild. He could have moved within two shots on 17 when I took a bogey, going twenty-five feet past the cup on my chip and needing two putts to get down. But Jack got into trouble himself, missing the green and needing two putts to get down for a bogey.

The 18th was about 600 yards, a par five. I hit my tee shot into a fairway bunker, played it out onto the middle of the fairway, and then caught a trap on my third shot right in front of the green. Nicklaus hit the green with two of the greatest shots I have ever seen. He two-putted for a birdie. I exploded out of the sand to within eight feet and sank the putt for the par and my 67.

It isn't often you beat Jack, who has to be among the greatest golfers of this or any era. All you need to do to fully appreciate his skills is realize that in 1962, as a rookie, he finished third in total money with $61,869. During his career he has finished first on the money list six times, second four times, third twice, and his low was as a fourth in 1970 at $142,149.

No one can say who the greatest golfer of all time is. Jack certainly has to be up among the best, and he no doubt is the best in the game today.

When I was a youngster in San Diego I watched Sam Snead every chance I could and tried to pattern my swing after his. I have always felt Sam hit a golf ball as well as anyone. I learned my swing more or less on my own, but Snead's rhythm was great, and I like to think that I picked up a tempo from him.

But the question of who is the best ever, creates nothing but arguments. I believe Jack is one of golf's finest technicians. He has all the skills with all the clubs, an ideal all-around player. Not only does he get great distance but he gets great control on his distance. There are some today who hit the ball as far or even farther but they might not always hit it where they're looking. And Nicklaus is one of the best putters the game has ever produced, especially when it means something.

What is most important is Jack's attitude. Although he has already won over fifty championships in his career he may put the number of titles won out of sight if he can maintain his incentive. I've never seen him when he is openly upset at himself or his game, and that kind of control makes for great determination. Jack may make two bad shots in a row, or a couple of double bogies, but he never quits. He just tries harder. That's what I admire most, because he doesn't need the money and he could just as easily pack it in and look ahead to the next week. Already he is nearly a million dollars ahead of Arnold Palmer in career money winnings and in his mid-thirties has to be at the prime of his game.

You can't say no one will ever surpass him because we thought when Arnold Palmer—who is cut of the same kind of cloth—was dominating the game that no one would duplicate some of the things that he did. Then along came Nicklaus. So now one of the many fine young golfers we have competing may rise to be as great or even greater. Nevertheless, Nicklaus has made his mark in history.

When you beat a player of Nicklaus's talent in a tournament you've got to believe you have played pretty well. And that's how I felt after winning the Thunderbird and that $25,000 prize money. I finished second in total winnings that year with $66,200 and Nicklaus was third at $61,869. Arnold Palmer led the way with $81,448.

You really realize how far golf has come when you start roaming through the record books. Paul Runyan was the leading money-winner back in 1934, and his total for the year was $6,767. You can take home more than that in a lot of tournaments today by finishing tenth or so.

Sometimes I wonder about relative values in golf. A fellow can win in one of the major events and get a very fine monetary award. In the last few years there has been some large ancillary income, mainly from special events connected with television.

I remember in the summer of 1962 going to Gleneagles, Scotland, to participate in the "Wonderful World of Golf" series sponsored by the Shell Oil Company. Our match was played over the King's Course at the Gleneagles Hotel, a beautiful resort in the Highlands area of Scotland.

We were to film the match and I was to play Eric Brown, who at the time had been the Scottish champion five of the previous seven years.

Those were the days before really mobile TV equipment, minicameras, etc. We were called at 6:00 A.M. and had to be out ready to play at 8:00 A.M.

On the first day we were on the course from 8:00 in the morning until 6:45 P.M. And after all that we had played only twelve holes. After every shot they had to move all the gear and we had to wait. We spent the time talking or, mostly, sitting on our golf bags.

It was July, with sunrise around 4:00 A.M. and sunset somewhere around 10 or 10:30 in the evening. The producer wouldn't let us play past 6:30 or 7:00 P.M. because he claimed the light wasn't good enough for the color film.

We couldn't hit between camera shots and sometimes half an hour or more would go by between our drive and our second shot. The toughest part after such a long wait was to drive down a narrow, well-bunkered fairway or hit a long wood to a well-trapped green.

As the match progressed under such tedious circumstances I found that I had to warm up five or six times more than I would have had we been playing tournament golf.

Gene Sarazen was the commentator and technical director for the show. The producer told us the series was costing Shell several hundred thousand dollars for production costs, air time, and other expenses. There was a gallery of three or four hundred people, as well as some extras. The extras were paid two pounds a day (then about $5.60) just to follow the match.

We finally wrapped it up the second day about noon. As I recall, we got $4,000 if we won and $2,000 if we lost, plus expenses. I think I won the match by a stroke. These TV shows are a little difficult to play but they all do an excellent job for the viewer.

With the new minicameras, remote towers, and wireless gear the technical coverage of golf had improved four years later in 1966 when I qualified to play in the World Series of Golf on TV. Only four were eligible. To make it you had to win the U.S. Open, the Masters, the PGA, or the British Open. If one of the four had won two of those titles, the Western Open was to be used and after that the Canadian Open to determine the participants.

Jack Nicklaus won both the Masters and the British Open and Billy Casper had won the Western and U.S. Open. In 1966 the Canadian Open was after the World Series so the 1965 Canadian Open, which I had won by a shot over Nicklaus for $20,000, had to be used. I don't know what they would have done to come up with four players if Jack had won instead of me.

So the four of us arrived at the Firestone Country Club in Akron for a 36-hole medal-play tournament. After thirty-six holes Allen Geiberger, who won the PGA, Nicklaus and I were all tied, and Billy Casper was a shot back. The three of us went to sudden death and on the 37th hole I birdied it to win. For that I received a check for $50,000—the most I had ever won in a single event at the time.

I didn't win a single tournament in 1966, yet I was the seventh man in money earned with $68,345 in twenty-four tournaments plus an additional $4,634 in pro-ams, for a total of $72,914—considerably behind Casper's leading sum of $121,944 in official money and $23,778 in unofficial earnings for a total of $145,723.

So you can see that $50,000 check for the World Series of Golf kicked me up to $122,914—pretty good for someone who was close a lot with seconds in the Tucson, Texas, and Memphis Opens and thirds in Phoenix, the PGA, the Philadelphia, and the Haig Scotch Mixed Foursome.

That is one of my problems. Once I get what I think is enough money for the year and am with my family at home, I lose incentive. I don't need all the money in the world. I've got a couple of expensive cars. I have one nice home and that's enough. You can only drive one car at a time and live in one home at a time.

Over the years I've turned down hundreds of things that could have made money for me. But they would also have required considerable time that I wasn't willing to take from my family.

A lot of the fellows, particularly the likes of Palmer, Nicklaus, Johnny Miller, and some of the others, have a great deal of outside income. I've done all right in this area but nothing like I could have if I were willing to take time away from home.

I've made a few investments, some of them good and some bad. I went into the clothing business in La Jolla one time. The store was located where Saks Fifth Avenue and some of the other fine shops in La Jolla do real well now, but we were there too early. When we were burglarized, the thieves got some garments but no cash. That we didn't have, and we finally went bankrupt.

Probably the best thing I had going for me was my original contract with Spalding. I was with them for the first eight years I was on the tour. We had a line of Gene Littler signature clubs and balls—and they sold a bundle of them. I got 3 percent of each sale and was making a good bit of money.

I have had a similar contract with Ram Corporation for several years, and we have enjoyed a fruitful relationship. I've also been under contract with Munsingwear for many years. I wear all their shirts, slacks, underwear and sweaters.

The last few years I've had a contract with Amana, the firm that makes refrigerators, freezers, radar ranges and other household appliances. The president of Amana, George Foerstner, had the idea of supplying a number of us with golf hats. All they have on them is the word *Amana* and we wear them all the time. I have been very fortunate along the way to have met many fine people, and the folks at Amana are among the very best, really super.

I've never had a business manager for any length of time nor have I ever demanded great sums up front to sign with firms such as Ram, Munsingwear, Amana, and others.

A lot of the fellows have been handled by Mark McCormack. I signed with him when he first started. Arnold Palmer has been very successful under his guidance, as have others. I've kind of dropped by the wayside, largely my fault. Mark would come to me with some good idea but I'd turn him down. It wasn't that I didn't want to work hard, playing exhibitions, for example, but it always came down to the same thing—I didn't want to be away from home.

I still have a casual connection with Mark, and every once in a while he will bring something to my attention to make a few extra dollars. I can't blame Mark for being frustrated with me. I would be too, but that's me.

When I first went on tour I represented Thunderbird Country Club in Palm Springs for two years. Later I played out of Singing Hills in San Diego and for about a year, the Dunes in Las Vegas. But for many years I've just been signing in as Gene Littler, La Jolla, California, since I have played at La Jolla Country Club from age eleven on.

A club affiliation requires the same thing as other endorsements—time. I've had several club offers over the years, but each one would have required me to be at the club for a month or more each year, and I was never willing to give up that kind of time.

I've never gotten rich from my outside income from golf but I have made a little. As a by-product of my ability to win on the tour it's nice. I welcome the opportunity it affords for a lot of the luxuries of life, and I feel fortunate to be making this kind of money on my free time.

Golf has really changed in every way over the years since I've been a touring pro. The courses are much better, and all the equipment is better; but the biggest change of all is in the amount of prize money awarded at each tournament.

I've got to give Arnold Palmer the most credit for that. With a lot of those phenomenal things he was doing he captivated galleries, the general public, and especially the TV audience.

Palmer was probably the most dynamic sports personality of these times. He was out there in front all the time and he sent those TV ratings out of sight. Then "Arnie's army"—as the media called it—seemed to assemble at every tournament. The public became enthralled with golf and things have just gone beyond anything I ever dreamed of.

I can remember the first time I won a $10,000 first prize. It was hard to believe that I'd really won that much money. Now you can look at $65,000 first prize—which I won in the 1974 and 1975 Japanese Masters—and not doubt that one of these days the figure may reach $100,000 for a one-week tournament. (Miller Barber won $100,000 at the first World Open at Pinehurst but that was over a two-week period.)

I'll never forget the players' meetings from the days when I first started. We might be playing for a total prize of $20,000 in a tournament (and that was big) and Freddie Haas would get up and preach about boosting the total to $50,000. Everybody thought Freddie was crazy. We'd ask him: "Who's going to put up $50,000?"

Freddie was so right. Few of the young players today have ever heard of Freddie Haas and his Easter-egg putter, but he was a visionary. Even Freddie's dreams have been surpassed with the $250,000 tournaments we have now.

I keep telling myself they can't go much higher, but I was wrong before. I never thought we'd be playing for $250,000. Somewhere downstream a few years farther there may be a million-dollar prize. Who knows?

19

Many people view tournament golf as a glamorous, happy-go-lucky life. In some respects it is. But to a person close to his home and his family it can also be very lonely.

I'm an early riser. My natural alarm sounds at 6:00 A.M., which can sometimes be convenient when you are on tour. You get out to the course early, get in a little practice, and can easily be ready to go as early as 8:00 A.M. Even if you have an 11:00 A.M. starting time it isn't hard to use the extra hours. You have a little more time to work on your game on the practice tee and putting green before teeing off.

The problem for me is what to do when you start at 8:00 A.M. and are through by noon. That leaves a lot of hours before 10:00 P.M. and sack time. Even though I usually spend some time after a round practicing, after a couple of hours I feel I should get some rest for the next day. It's fine in the summers when Shirley, Curt, and Suzanne—or at least Shirley—are along. But when you're out there alone those hours drag by forever.

Some of the guys think I have pretty funny ways of eating up that time. Of course, I read the want ads in every city looking for old cars. More often than not, however, there is nothing in them that intrigues me so I move along to my next hobby.

I love to visit hock shops. My primary interest is old golf clubs. The old drivers and old woods are made from finely seasoned persimmon wood that used to be subjected to an oil-hardening process.

One of the hock shops I like to visit is in Augusta, Georgia. I bought a driver there years ago that is a classic, and in 1974 picked up a set of four matched woods. That shop has a good line of tools, and I've picked up a bunch of hand tools and a variety of other things. I've also bought some hand power tools —a flat sander, a spray gun and one time a disc sander mounted on a table.

Some of the airline clerks look at me a little strangely when I check in with a huge bag of clubs with my name all over it and a spray gun, for example. I found one in a pawn shop in Phoenix and when I checked it in along with my luggage I'm sure the counter man must have wondered about my sanity.

I spend hours refinishing my woods. If I have a driver I like real well, I don't trust anyone to work on it. Just a little slip of a file, for example, and the club will never be the same.

Once I realized I had to have surgery I knew something would have to compensate for the muscle loss on my left side. I didn't know how much until I was able to really let out on a drive.

During my recuperation period when I would take a break from restoring Shirley's white Rolls, I began to try a set of clubs with graphite shafts. They were relatively new on the market then. I had heard about them but had never really had the time to test them out.

After two or three weeks of playing—once I could, after surgery—I became convinced they gave me added distance that I now felt I needed if I was going to be able to compete as well as in the past.

Over a period of weeks I tried a number of shafts with different flex ratings. A graphite shaft is at least an ounce and a half lighter than a steel shaft, giving you a lighter overall club even though it is necessary to add some weight to the head. If you can swing a lighter club such as a graphite faster than you can a club with a steel shaft, the ball should go farther. And it does, I'm convinced. I started out using just the woods but am now using irons, too.

The graphite club shafts I used are made by Aldila Precision Golf Products here in San Diego. An old friend of mine, Dr. John Moler, now retired from dentistry, is president of the firm and Glenn Campbell and Andy Williams are investors in it. I think it is really going to be something. I know they have really helped my long game.

The company is getting into other areas of sports equipment now. My son, Curt, is playing with a new graphite tennis racquet they recently put on the market, and he loves it.

Another item I've put together since my surgery is a weighted driver. I felt I had to have something I could swing indoors to redevelop whatever muscle structure I had left and strengthen the ones I would use for golf.

I took an old driver and cut the shaft off to about the length of a two-iron so I could swing it indoors in motel rooms when I'm on tour and not be ripping into the ceiling and knocking down light fixtures. I weighted the clubhead as much as possible and filled the whole shaft with lead. It weighs about three or four pounds. Considering the fact that my driver weighs less than thirteen ounces, it's not hard to believe that, after you swing that weighted club around a few times, you can feel it. I believe it is going to build up my hands, wrists, forearms and the back muscles that I need. It also boosts the weight of my bag a lot!

Since I've had surgery, I have watched my diet very carefully. Now I have what I call my cooking suitcase, which contains an electric frying pan, some silverware, a cooking spoon, a sharp knife, and some medium-sized plastic bowls.

I try to find a place to stay that has kitchen facilities, which is sometimes hard to do. Once I get to the tournament city I go shopping. I usually take oat groats along with me to have for breakfast and buy whatever I want to eat daily. If we do have a kitchen I can buy for a day or two. I pick up a package of paper plates so I don't have to do any dishes.

I usually have a good-sized breakfast and pass up lunch. Dinner is my meal for the day. I'll pick up some fresh vegetable —zucchini (I'm big on that), string beans, or some other favorite—and I'll get some romaine lettuce or head lettuce, Bibb lettuce or whatever looks freshest. Then I chop it all; cut in a carrot, cucumber, some celery; add a sliced tomato and half an avocado; top it with a little lemon and oil—and that's my salad.

By the time I'm through with that I'll toss a piece of meat into the electric frying pan and in a minute or two will have a broiled steak in natural juices. About the third night I won't have any meat at all and instead will just have a huge salad and vegetables.

Most of the pros don't know I do my own cooking. I don't tell any of them because they would probably think I was pretty weird. But I am so convinced that diet is vital to good health that we have turned our family eating habits completely around since my cancer surgery.

I don't smoke and I don't drink, and now I'm on a health-food kick. I call it my "try-to-eat-right" kick. After I got out of Mercy Hospital Shirley and I read a book entitled *Food Is Your Best Medicine*.

I went to see the author, Dr. Henry Bieler, and talked to him at length about diet. He believes that overconsumption of animal protein is harmful to good health. We went on a very low protein diet, and, boom, in two weeks I went from 165 to 147. I can't ever remember weighing less than 165. A lot of my friends kept telling me I looked awful—so skinny that I went back to Dr. Bieler and we added some protein and potatoes.

What I do now is try to eat a lot less meat than I used to. At most I eat it only once a day, whereas it used to be three times. I eat nothing with white sugar; avoid anything made of white flour products; and try not to eat any processed foods.

About the only time I use milk is on my oat groats at breakfast. I've given up drinking it. And given up the only thing I really miss—ice cream. I was a super ice-cream eater.

No one knows the cause of cancer but I'm trying to do everything possible that might keep it in an arrested condition. And since so many people feel that diet is important I'm going to adhere to mine.

My frying pan and utensils go along in the summer when Shirley and the kids join in. The only difference is that Shirley does the cooking. She's a lot better than I am (although I'm not bad on the backyard barbecue).

Being on the tour is much more pleasant when my family is along. None of us like suitcase life but I'm never lonesome like I am when I'm out alone.

It's great to have Shirley take over all the details, too. She arranges for all our accommodations ahead of time, lines up the rental car, pays all the bills, handles all the correspondence, confirms space on our next airline flight and just leaves me to think solely about golf.

I will say that traveling is much better since the airlines have the wide-bodied jets. Nowadays I have a large suitcase I fold my clothes into, my kitchen case, and my bag of clubs. I used to carry a hanging case for slacks and suits but with the new double-knits there's no problem of pressing so I abandoned it. I pack all my underwear and some sweaters in with the kitchen gear to keep it from rattling around. Nothing is breakable so that is not a worry.

In the over twenty years I have been on tour I've seldom lost anything. Oh, I've had my clubs or suitcase not come off the plane a number of times. Either they weren't loaded aboard or they went to a wrong city. But I have never been forced to tee off in tournament play without my clubs, although I have played several practice rounds with borrowed sticks. Only once have I lost any clubs for good. In 1974, coming out of the British Open in Liverpool, someone heisted my two-iron and my four-iron. I guess they wanted them for souvenirs or something.

We had a funny experience in 1975 after I had won the

Bing Crosby. We flew home from San Francisco, barely making the plane, and got up early the next morning to repack and take off for Honolulu and the Hawaiian Open.

The phone rang off the wall all morning because I had just won the Crosby. Along about eleven o'clock we just had to take it off the hook or we were never going to make our 1:00 P.M. plane.

As we packed a bag we'd haul it out to the kitchen where it would be right next to the door to the garage and the car. When the packing was all done, we grabbed everything, put the bags and my clubs in the trunk, and hung up the phone. It was already ringing away as we were driving out. We barely made the plane. Waiting for our luggage in Honolulu, I checked the bags as they came off. One clothes case, two clothes cases, one golf bag. Then nothing more. No kitchen bag. We had had them check the plane's baggage compartment when I realized that the kitchen bag was still over in one corner of the kitchen at home.

That's where my friend Hank Wohlers came to our rescue. Hank always brings in all our mail and sorts out the important things to forward to us on tour, among many other helpful tasks. This time he had to pick up the kitchen kit and take it to the airline to be sent to us on the next plane.

The only thing we've lost and never recovered was Shirley's suitcase. Coming back one year from the Ryder Cup matches in Houston, it just vanished. I guess somebody just put the arm on it. Airlines only insure bags for $500, and normally, that's fine. But this time Shirley had bought several new dresses, and she had her jewelry in the suitcase along with everything else so it was quite a loss.

My wardrobe on tour is relatively simple compared to most: about six pairs of slacks, golf shirts and sweaters to match, my rain gear and umbrella which are in my golf bag. I may possibly include one dress suit if I know of a rather formal dinner I may have to attend if there is no way out, and a sport coat or two. I always take a couple pairs of street shoes and two pair of golf shoes.

I alternate my golf shoes, wearing a different pair every day. Johnson & Murphy give me my shoes as part of my endorsement of their line. Over a year I have them make me eight or ten pairs. In view of the weather we sometimes encounter and the rough wear we give shoes, that will usually carry me through the season. The worst thing is rain. When it really pours it takes a couple days for a pair of shoes to dry out. If there are back-to-back rainy days you're playing in wet feet.

At each country club the Tournament Players Division sets up a finance committee which will cash checks for the players. Over the years there have been a few who bounced a check or two. If they persist they get bounced.

Shirley and I mail any winning checks to our bank in San Diego and then write checks as we need them on the road. Years ago I tried using Traveler's Checks but you'd need another suitcase to carry them in so we had to abandon that.

The tour is easier physically now than when we started, but it's not easier on the pocketbook. When we were trailering back in the '50s we could live real well for everything on a couple hundred dollars a week, including meals, entry and caddy fee. Now, depending on how far we have to travel, I expect to spend somewhere between $600 and $1000 per week, and I don't throw money around. The kitchen kit keeps my food bill a little less than if I were eating out, and I eat a lot better.

There's just one thing I'd like to add to my travel gear—my videotape machine. It lets you see instantly what you are doing wrong—whatever you want to check about your game, even to zeroing in on your grip or your swing. Shirley can operate the machine and it can be played back through its own little set or a home TV receiver. I know of several club pros who use it constantly as a teaching device. And of course many of the baseball and football teams have monitors in various locations in the park to check on their players' performance. But it's too heavy to be practical to take along even though I have a travel case for it.

Oh, well. I read the other day where Dick Williams, manager of the California Angels, had his focused on his outfielders to see if they were getting the right jump on the ball. When he called for the tape the operator had blown it—he had missed just the play Dick needed to see.

No one needs to tell you when you're having a problem, but it took two years for me to find out from Paul Runyan what was wrong. Videotaping might cut the time down a bit . . . hopefully like to about ten minutes.

20

On tour you acquire acquaintances over the years that you may see at each tour stop. Some become very warm personal friends.

Years ago when I played in Kansas City we met the Bryans—Ted and Winnie and their three children—Barbara, Jim, and Tim. Ted was then an executive with Folger's Coffee Co. Over the years we have become very, very close friends.

Ted's retired now and living in Florida so whenever we play in the area the Bryans are around. One of their sons, Jim, is an ophthalmologist in the Los Angeles area, and his parents try to arrange visits that correspond with golf tournaments like the Los Angeles Open, the Crosby, and the Tournament of Champions at La Costa.

Ted can almost recall my tournament rounds better than I can. He's a pretty good needler, too. One time I'd shanked a ball quite badly, and as he walked by me he said, "I can hit 'em that way."

I didn't say a word; I just handed him the club. Only trouble is that he talks better than he scores, but it did one good thing: it relaxed me and I went on to have a pretty good round.

Two of my closest friends in San Diego are Hank and Bert

Wohlers. Hank is a former naval officer, now retired, who plays quite a game of golf. He was a scratch golfer when he was playing a lot. After his retirement he turned pro for something to do. Now he works as an assistant up at the Torrey Pines Country Club where they play the Andy Williams San Diego Open.

Hank spent a lot of time with me after my surgery. In fact, he helped do a lot of the tough paint-stripping on the white Rolls Shirley drove most of the time.

He opens up Torrey Pines, and that's early. They're in line at dawn waiting to tee off. A lot of people from the Los Angeles area drive down to play. Some of them come in those big campers and sleep in the parking lot so they're ready when the sun's up.

Because of those hours, Hank is usually through about noon and that's when he'll show up to help me on the cars. He's pretty mechanical and likes to tinker as much as I do.

When there is no one left at home in the summer—the times that both Curt and Suzanne go with us—Hank and his wife, Bert, come by to check on the house. They'll water the house plants and the areas of the yard that aren't on the sprinkler system, and Hank takes care of the mail. Perhaps once a week he packages up what looks important—utility bills, other bills, etc.—and forwards them to our next tour stop. We leave him an itinerary so he knows where we'll be week to week. All the unimportant mail he leaves at home. That looks like a mountain when we return after six weeks or so. It's hard to repay that kind of friendship, and we feel very fortunate to have known the Wohlerses all these years.

We have also developed very close friendships with the Dave Taylors, the Don Drinkards, and the Dee Replogles. The Taylors, Drinkards, and Replogles are the only friends we ever stay with out on the tour besides the Bryans. The Taylors live in Pebble Beach where we stay during the Crosby, and Dave was the one who got me interested in restoring Rolls Royces. The Drinkards have us as houseguests each year for the Memphis Open. The Replogles' home is where we stayed when I won the U.S. Amateur. We stay with them when an event is near their home in Oklahoma City.

The Wohlerses, the Taylors, the Bryans, the Drinkards, the Replogles—they're all wonderful people and are typical of the friends you make over the years in professional golf.

We always worry when we're gone that something will happen to the house. The only time it did was in the summer of 1973. Curt had been with us for four weeks and wanted to go home to play a little tennis. We had a couple more weeks to go before we came back. He had been in the house all evening but was eating and sleeping at Mom's. About bedtime he hopped in his T-Bird and went over to sleep, even forgetting to take his wallet that had a few dollars in it and his watch.

Sometime during the night someone took a monkey wrench or something and just twisted the doorknob and walked in. They were very selective in what they took. All my medals, which included medals for the U.S. Open, U.S. Amateur, and several tour wins; the beautiful gold money clips they give you for playing in the Ryder Cup matches—I think I had six; several watches I had won as prizes in my amateur days, including a beautiful Rolex that Frankie Laine gave me for winning the Tournament of Champions; some of Shirley's jewelry; and Curt's watch and the few dollars he had in his wallet.

They didn't take any of the sterling trophies or flat silver nor any of the TV sets or radios. It's funny. All the things they took were gold and heavily engraved. I don't know what they could do with it except melt it down. As soon as we got home I had the whole place wired with a security system.

That's like closing the barn door after the horse is a mile or two down the path, but now if anyone so much as breathes the system is activated and the police are there.

It seems nothing today is safe anyplace. At Stanford one time Curt and his friends decided to go down and get a pizza. They drove his Mustang. When they came out he put the key in the ignition to start it and nothing happened.

Curt opened the hood and saw that the battery had been lifted while they were eating. That's why he decided to leave the T-Bird at home.

My caddy always keeps a close eye on my bag at tournaments. Since I bring along only two extra clubs—a driver and a putter—if someone were to help himself to an iron or two while the bag was stashed outside the dressing room I'd be in deep trouble. You can always buy clubs in the pro shop, of course, but playing with them would be like playing with strangers.

Caddies are important people to a golf pro. Primo Antoniotti, who originally worked for Doug Ford, has been my caddy for several years. When Doug began to taper off playing the tour, Primo asked if he could work for me. He is a fine man, in his sixties, and lives in New Jersey.

After my surgery, as I began trying to get myself ready to go back on the tour he came out and spent a month at the house. We'd practice every day. Each time it was a little longer and he was a great help. I couldn't go long at a time but I'd practice three or four times each day. Primo would shag for me, and then when we weren't working out he'd lend a hand around the house.

Primo is a super guy with a super attitude, which is not something you can say about a lot of the men carrying. Some of them are lazy; some get disgusted when you miss a putt or blow a shot. Primo never does that. Most important thing, he is reliable. Sometimes he will drive another pro's car or hop a ride to the next tournament with some other caddy driving a car, or if going to the west coast he will fly.

Caddies pace off the course to get distances from various geographical markers like a tree or a sprinkler head, something that will stay fixed. And I always check those distances in a practice round. Then each day Primo checks where the pins have been placed on the greens, and we add the two together for the correct overall distance.

I've always made it clear to whoever caddies for me that I will select the club. I have never wanted a caddy to hand me an iron, a sand wedge or any club as if he is suggesting what I should use. That's my job and I know best what shot I want to play, and with which club.

At some tournaments, you know, you can't use your own caddy. You have to use a caddy from that club. That's the way it is at the U.S. Open, the Masters and at the Western Open where they use students from the Chick Evans college scholarship program.

Most players pay their caddies around 4 or 5 percent of their earnings. That's about what Primo ends up with, so you can see that the better I do the better he does.

One of the big problems of tournament golf and one that has bugged me for years is the continued slow pace of play. There are still too many slow players, even after all the publicity the problem has received. I know that large galleries tend to slow down play but the real problem is the player who doesn't plan ahead and takes forever to judge and hit a shot.

It's a matter the Players Association discusses every year. There have been a lot of suggestions. A time clock like the 24-second clock used in the National Basketball Association has been tried. I don't recall how long we had it but I liked it real well and it seemed to work. I don't know whatever happened to the idea.

I think we have to do something. Galleries don't want to watch forever while some player does all that pacing, looks over the green for grain and whatever, or checks the wind with bits of flying grass.

Just by the slow pace of play I feel I have slowed down, although I would prefer to play fast. When I'm over at La Jolla Country Club I'll play eighteen with three others in three to three and a half hours if the course isn't crowded, and I never feel rushed.

I hope some solution can be reached. I really feel it might be the one thing that could kill the game. The slowest man, if he's starting early, sets the pace for the pack.

Patience is the greatest asset a golfer can have. Look at Ben Hogan. You could never really tell looking at Hogan whether he was shooting 60 or 80. Jack Nicklaus is the same way. Both of them just play their game, keep swinging away with that great abundance of patience.

God gave me a slow boiling point. I seldom show anger outwardly. That doesn't mean that I'm not mad at myself inside because often I am. But you lose command of yourself and therefore command of your game if you take your anger out physically.

I've never broken a golf club around a tree or a water pipe —not that I haven't wanted to a time or two in my twenty plus years—but I don't think it is good for me as an individual or for the image of golf.

I remember a column Jim Murray wrote in the *Los Angeles Times* several years ago. I was playing in the San Diego Open, my hometown, and it was not too long after all my swing troubles. I still remember the little headline on his column: "Littler Joins Club—Loses Temper"

I talked with Jim about it. I had an explanation, but the incident still shouldn't have happened because it was seen by the world on television. I hadn't won a tournament in too long a time, I was in my hometown, and I had hit a nine-iron pitch real well. The only trouble was that the ball nicked the limb of an overhanging eucalyptus branch on the way to what I felt was going to be a very fine shot. When it came down short of the green I just buried the head of the nine-iron in the fairway, and, as Jim said, gave it that "why me" look. I finished only a stroke behind Nicklaus, the eventual winner, so that was a pretty important shot at the time.

I don't think I have buried a club since. I try not to. Over the years I have broken a club or two hitting a tree when I could do nothing else but hit the tree with the shaft of the club.

You can replace a club broken during the course of play if you have another one but, as I said, I only carry a spare driver and putter. When I break an iron I just have to wait and have it reshafted at the earliest convenience.

Of course, I have enough clubs at home for half the tour players. Over in the corner of the garage next to the Rolls Town Sedan that's waiting for me to restore, I have a club storage bin. It's really a big wooden box on wheels and just full of clubs that I'm not currently using.

I have the full set of clubs I used to win the U.S. Open in 1961, the irons I won the U.S. Amateur with in Oklahoma City, a lot of Aldila graphite-shafted clubs and a lot of Ram equipment. There are also many spare drivers mixed in with a hundred or so putters, among them a spare Zebra, that I may some day use.

I guess I'm what you could call a collector of things—clubs, cars, tools, important things to me like the awards and honors I have received over the years which we keep along with important trophies in our trophy cases in the den.

A lot of nice things have come my way over the years and I truly appreciated them. A special one was in 1961, the year I won the Open, when I was named Athlete of the Year in California by the writers for Associated Press. As I recall Elgin Baylor, the absolutely superstar of the Los Angeles Lakers, was second, with Orlando Cepeda of the Giants, and Jerry Barber, who had won the PGA, next. Some of the others who got votes were big people like Archie Moore, Sandy Koufax, Willie Mays.

As I told the reporters who interviewed me, when I read the names of those superstars, I was truly grateful for the honor I had just received.

21

The line between being super, great, good and bad is too fine to measure. But if I could find the formula and bottle it, I'll guarantee I'd never have a worry again in the world—financially, that is.

Someone asked me after I had won the Phoenix Open in 1969—one of two championships I acquired that year—how I could put together four rounds of golf like that. That is a secret I'd like to know too.

I shot rounds of 69–66–62–66—263 at the Arizona Country Club, 21 under par. It was the lowest total score during the entire tour in 1969 and most strokes under par for the year.

A lot of us played fine golf those four days. Miller Barber, Don January, and Billy Maxwell were only two shots back at 265 and three others—Ray Floyd, Terry Wilcox, and Jack Ewing—were another two back at 267.

The win was worth $20,000, and only two weeks before I took second in the Andy Williams San Diego Open to Jack Nicklaus by a shot at 285 for another $17,100.

In the first week in April, playing in the Greater Greensboro Open at Sedgefield Country Club, Orville Moody, Julius Boros, Tom Weiskopf, and I tied at the end of seventy-two holes at 274. We went to sudden death and I won it on the first extra hole. There was a difference of $20,000 between winning and tying for second. I'll always take $32,000 to $12,373.34 if I can.

Phoenix and Greensboro were my only wins in 1969 but I finished sixth in total earnings at $112,737.27. That was the first time I had gone over $100,000 in official winnings in a single year. Prior to that I had finished second in 1962 with $66,200, and my next highest money year was seventh in 1966 with $68,345.

I use those statistics to illustrate how rapidly the tour escalated in a few years in potential dollar winnings. The whole pyramid, I believe, began with Arnold Palmer's rise to the top. From 1934 when Paul Runyan topped the official all-time leading money-winner list with $6,767, there was a steady, gradual increase until 1962.

In that year Arnold was lead man at $81,448. He repeated in 1963 but with $128,230—the first six-figure man in golf history. From 1963 on Jack Nicklaus never earned less than $100,000 and neither did Arnold, until after the 1971 campaign when he began to devote more and more of his time to business interests. Through the 1975 season a total of forty-five tour members have won $100,000 one or more years. Nicklaus, with thirteen, is at the head of the class.

To illustrate further the increase in the growth of tour purses, when I began in 1954 we played for a grand total of $600,819 in thirty-seven events. The estimate for 1976 is forty-nine sanctioned tournaments worth $9,073,450.

When you play with statistics you can come up with a lot of incredible facts. For example, Byron Nelson has some achievements on the tour that no one may ever match. He won eleven consecutive tournaments between March 11 and August 4, 1945, and all he earned was $63,335.66. In that same year he had nineteen consecutive rounds under 70. He won eighteen tournaments during the year, and in one span during the 1940s Lord Byron was in the money 113 straight times.

In all the years of professional golf going back to the turn of the century only seven men have won a single event in three consecutive years. Willie Anderson started it all off winning the United States Open in 1903–1904–1905. Walter Hagen is the king of them all—he won the PGA four years running between 1924 and 1927.

Ralph Guldahl took the Western Open in 1936–1938; Billy Casper the Portland Open 1959–1961; Jack Nicklaus the Walt Disney World Golf Classic 1971–1973; a fellow named Littler the Tournament of Champions 1955–1957. Only Arnold Palmer has accomplished the feat twice, winning the Texas Open 1960–1962 and the Phoenix Open 1961–1963.

An achievement I am quite proud of is becoming one of the tour's million-dollar winners, twenty years and a month after becoming eligible for my first official prize money. That first red-letter date came in the Kansas City Open August 1, 1954, when I tied for second place and won $1,950.

I turned millionaire golfer on September 1, 1974, in the $250,000 Tournament Players Championship, played at the Atlanta Country Club. I finished fourth behind Jack Nicklaus with rounds of 72–69–69–67—277 and won $11,750. In that twenty-year, one-month period I played in 487 tournaments and won 25 before I hit a million. (See appendix for millionaire list.)

At the time I was the eighth man in history to go over the mark, and I broke it by $8,454. I remember telling the media at the time what a nice feeling it was to join the club. But I also feel the accomplishment should be put in the proper perspective.

It really doesn't mean all that much when you consider that the likes of Sam Snead and Ben Hogan aren't on the list. The most Snead ever won in his best year as a leading money-winner of a single season was $35,758 in 1950, and Hogan's high as leading money-winner was in 1948 at $32,112. Why, one year—1940—Ben led the pack with $10,655.

I earned a lot of my million back in the days when $2,000 was first prize. And Snead and Hogan were playing in events where maybe $500 or $1,000 was first prize. It takes a lot of first prizes at that figure to make a million.

For example, I have played in recent years in the Pacific

Masters Invitational Golf Tournament in Tokyo. In 1974 I won it beating Bert Yancey by five strokes. We played it in very rainy conditions all week. My shoes never got dry even though I brought an extra pair along.

The total purse was $300,000 in U.S. dollars. I've forgotten what the figure was in yen but it was an awesome sum. Besides the $65,000 first prize, there was also a daily prize for the leader of each round. I tied for the lead on Saturday and won it on Sunday—shooting 69s in a driving rain—so I won another $3,000.

When Shirley, Suzanne, Curt, and I left Tokyo, it was with $68,000 in a check, not in cash dollars and certainly not in yen. Just think—that is more than double Hogan's leading money-winning year and almost double Snead's.

Playing in the Pacific Masters is a picnic. If you don't like to hear cameras click you had better stay home. It seems as if every person in the gallery is a photographer, and they must take thousands of pictures on every shot. It's just like machine-gun fire, and it never stops. I wonder if they really have film in all those cameras. If they do, they shoot up a fortune in film every hole.

The Pacific Masters will always remain in my memory, not for my wins in 1974 and 1975 but for my appearance in October 1972. It was the first tournament I played in after my surgery. When I stepped up to that first tee I just said a little thanks to the Lord that I was able to swing a club well enough to be called to the first tee instead of the last.

I played in three other tournaments on the tour after that, and a total of eleven for the year. Not counting my fifth place in Tokyo, worth $4,800, I won $11,119, or just a wee bit above the $8,327 I won my first year on tour. But I was happy to settle for just driving off that first tee in Tokyo. It had been a long road back, and when I hit that first drive I didn't know if it was going to be a long one or go skidding off into the gallery packed in so tightly around the fairway.

When I played in Tokyo—and the same has since been true all over the world—I received great pleasure from having people come up to me and say they're cancer victims or have someone in the family who is, and that I have been an inspiration to them. They tell me how important it is to see me hit a golf ball, how it helps them or others.

It helps me when it helps them. I draw from it. Some day the cancer could still creep back again, but you can't live in fear. I might be hit with it someplace else tomorrow, but so might the person walking beside me. We made up our minds in our family that we were going to live a normal life—one day at a time.

Even though I thought I was aware of the total implications of Dr. Isenhour's discovery and all the confirming diagnosis, looking back on it I can see I wasn't totally in tune with the road ahead. Not until much later—after I was back playing subpar golf and winning here and there—did all the physicians admit their greatest fears.

"We never thought you would play tournament golf again," my friend Dr. Dave Freeman told me.

Dr. Isenhour, the only other golfer among the medical group involved, was often a partner of Dad's at La Jolla. He too felt I had little chance of playing competitively. He and Dave Freeman were a little more familiar with my problem because they were good weekend golfers themselves.

After I had played so well in Tokyo—I was three under par for the tournament at 281—Dr. Isenhour went into some detail concerning his fears. Golfers have always regarded the game as a lefthanded one for those who play righthanded. So did Dr. Isenhour, but his fears were medical and mine only reflected the golfer's viewpoint.

He feels that the muscles on the left side provide the control factor on the backswing and the power on the follow-through. His fear was that the flaring of the scapula—which seems necessary for proper swing control—would not assist for a grooved swing.

Those fears on my part and on the part of the medical group faded with my almost daily improvement. Muscles and nerves left on that side compensated and took over for those lost in the radical surgery.

Dr. Jesse Bowers, a physiatrist who created my rehabilitation program and supervised the therapy, has been surprised at the dramatic way the remaining muscles have compensated under rehabilitation.

He continually tested my muscles to see how progress continued. I remember his telling me one day: "Gene, your body is cheating to compensate automatically for the missing muscle (*serratus anterior*) to prevent winging of the shoulder blade." I'm not much on human anatomy but he told me that the *trapezius* (a large muscle in the back) developed to where it held the shoulder blade in place. What was left of the *pectoralis major*—the large muscle in the chest—stabilized the front of the shoulder to provide the forward motion.

What concerned Dr. Bowers most was the absence of a muscle called the *latissimus dorsi*—the muscle you use to chop wood, for example—which gives a golfer the powerful downward motion and pull needed for hitting the ball hard. He's still amazed that I'm able to hack my way out of deep rough and so am I. Sometimes I don't, but my play out of the real deep grass has improved bit by bit. Somewhere some muscles which haven't been identified yet are taking over.

Every three months I go back in for a complete examination. So far everything has been in my favor. I hope I continue to get reports like this, but Dr. Groesbeck, who gives me the checkup, and Dr. Lee Monroe at Scripps Clinic will not quote time statistics. They only tell me one thing: "Gene, the longer you go without a recurrence the better your chances."

They won't give me that five-year figure you hear so often in cancer cases: after five years you're home free. They don't believe you can blanket patients with a statistical average.

The full impact of what cancer could mean really hit me hard in 1975 during the Westchester Classic in Rye, New York. During the second round we got word from California that one of the bright young prospects on the tour—Gary Sanders—had died.

During the Western Open in Oak Brook, Illinois, Gary had discovered a lump under his left armpit while toweling off. He flew back to Los Angeles and entered UCLA Medical Center where doctors removed a small tumor from that arm for a biopsy.

He had been scheduled to reenter UCLA Medical Center

the following Monday but before then he died from a malignant melanoma with the primary site undetermined. It was widespread in the axillary lymph nodes, the right lung, and the cerebellum, according to the autopsy. Gary's death was a shock to all of us who knew him and had played with him.

It was most shocking to me since I had had a long talk with him the week before about his plans for the operation. He'd thought he would be playing again in three weeks.

I've always been thankful that Dr. Isenhour was an insistent, demanding man.

My admonition to all is that wherever there is any question you follow your doctor's advice. Although negative reports of a malignancy are the kind you want to hear, even a positive one, if it is early enough, leaves you with hope.

My whole experience with cancer has been overwhelming to me. Overwhelming that I'm alive. Overwhelming that I play golf. Overwhelming that I play competitively and can win from time to time.

But the most overwhelming thing of all has been people. When you are in the public eye as a golfer is, you get to feeling that there are so many phony people. But I've certainly found there are an awful lot of good, sincere folks around. They encouraged me. They prayed for me. In long letters, they cited their own experiences.

They, as much as all the medical men and women, strengthened my personal desire to make it back in competitive golf.

I became convinced, thanks to all the letters and personal messages, that if I could become a tournament winner again after what had happened it would give other people afflicted with cancer a lot of hope that they, too, could make it back.

That was my goal in golf. I only hope that I can be an inspiration to many others.

22

Every once in a while some of us will get to talking about great golf courses in the world. And there are many, many of them. Some of us have courses we like better than others and some consider one the best of all.

I have no problem naming some of the truly fine courses in this country. My play in foreign events has been too limited for me to lay claim to any expertise there. I'll leave that to golfers like Gary Player who seem to be constantly circling the world.

Among my favorites—and not necessarily in any order—are Oakland Hills in Birmingham, Michigan, where I won the Open in 1961; Baltusrol near Springfield, New Jersey; Pine Valley in western New Jersey, one of the truly beautiful and tough courses; Riviera in Los Angeles where they now hold the Los Angeles Open again; the north course at Los Angeles Country Club; Augusta National; and two of my all-time favorites, Pebble Beach and Cypress Point on the Monterey Peninsula in northern California. These are only a few that come to mind. There are many other outstanding courses.

I guess for downright beauty as well as for being a stern test of golf Pine Valley rates among the best. It's just vast areas of

171

sand, a lot of trees, a little bit of water, and a small amount of grass sprinkled in between. I love to play that course.

Augusta is a nice place to play golf but I feel it could be an even greater course if it weren't so wide open. It's a long hitter's course, giving that type of player quite an advantage, but there are many demanding shots required into the greens. There's no question that the Masters is one of the world's finest tournaments.

I suppose if I were forced to make a decision and play in only one geographic area the rest of my life it would have to be at Monterey. Pebble Beach and Cypress Point provide two of the greatest tests of golfing skill anywhere, along with incomparable beauty.

When I grew up playing golf the stress was on hitting the ball straight. Only after you had learned to do that did you attempt to hit it longer. Now the emphasis seems to be on length almost entirely. I see today's golf architecture as the reason.

Most courses are somewhere over seven thousand yards, and accuracy is not as important as distance. While I believe that a player who is long off the tee should have an advantage, that should only be true if he hits the ball as straight as the shorter-hitting man.

I once sat down and figured out about how many miles I've walked in my lifetime on golf courses if they are averaged out at around seven thousand yards long. It is an astronomical distance. You walk probably six miles a day just playing eighteen holes. I probably play at least three hundred rounds a year counting tournaments, exhibitions, practice and charity events.

That comes out to about eighteen hundred miles a year, times twenty years is thirty-six thousand miles. From the time I was eleven or twelve it was nothing for me to play thirty-six holes a day and sometimes forty-five. So it is possible that I might have doubled that figure just playing golf.

Adding it all together, I believe I figured that I had walked about seventy thousand miles, give or take a few, and that's a lot of mileage.

One thing about golf, however, is that I haven't heard many

of the pros talking about their legs giving out, as do baseball players or basketball players or professionals in some of the other sports. I would guess the biggest physical problem in golf is in the back. But with any professional athlete, I think the thing that goes first is his enthusiasm for what he is doing and his concentration.

All kinds of golfers have back problems. The violence of a golf swing has a great deal to do with it. I developed a little bit of a disc problem the last year or so in the low back but the doctors feel it can be controlled with exercise to strengthen the stomach and back muscles.

In 1975 at the Crosby I was out playing a practice round on Tuesday and my back was hurting so much by about the fourth hole I felt I shouldn't play any more. We were staying with our friends the Dave Taylors, who have a hydrotherapy pool about seven by four feet that they keep around 107 or 108 degrees. I staggered back to their home and climbed into that warm water and just let it massage my back fifteen or twenty minutes two or three times that day.

That really saved me. I was in the tub before and after every round. I had been trying to win the Crosby all my life, and if the Taylors hadn't had that tub I wouldn't have been able to play in the tournament and one of the great moments of my life wouldn't have been.

The new putter Dave created had a lot to do with realizing that dream too.

I had just finished playing in the Tucson Open where I had putted terribly. Nothing seemed to drop. Nor did any of the putts seem to be stroked right. I was desperate for a putter. Dave, a fine machinist and inventor, had just finished making this putter by hand. He called it the "Zebra." When I picked it up, I liked the way it felt.

On Tuesday night I said, "Let me try that putter tomorrow." The tournament was due to start on Thursday. We stuck a grip on it and went out to practice with it. It felt pretty good, and when I got back to the Taylors after the practice round, we went out in his shop and did a little more remodeling.

It's the best-balanced putter I ever used, and has about eight vertical lines from the face to the heel, which theoretically makes it easier to line up the face with the hole than it is with the standard method.

Well, I must have lined up well because I won the Crosby in probably the finest weather the tournament has ever had. My score was 280, four strokes ahead of Hubie Green. It was my twenty-sixth career tournament win in twenty-plus years and in some respects a most memorable win.

It was my second major win after my surgery, and it came on a tough collection of courses—Spyglass Hill, Cypress Point and the jewel, Pebble Beach. My win in July 1973 in the St. Louis Children's Hospital Golf Classic still stands out as a great moment of my life but certainly the course didn't offer the test of the ones at Monterey Peninsula.

The Bing Crosby National Pro-Am is one of the great tournaments. While it may not quite have the prestige of the U.S. Open, the Masters, or the PGA, in my book it ranks right up there close to them and any other classic tournament in the world.

I was leading the Crosby by four strokes going into the final round. There once was a day when that was a comfortable lead and you could go out there and play a little conservatively and win. But now a lead like that doesn't mean a thing. We've got all those players out there—Johnny Miller is a prime example—who are capable of shooting a 61 or in the low 60s on any round on any golf course. That means you had better play hard for some birdies if you're going to hold onto a lead and win.

Often I've been asked my preference—playing from behind to win or playing from in front? It's much easier to win a tournament coming from behind. There is far more pressure if you are out in front unless, of course, you're way out in front by ten or twelve strokes. A one-shot lead means nothing. Neither does two or three. Four shots or so is good but only if you play a fine last round.

The first three rounds of the Crosby are played on a rotating basis on all three courses. The final eighteen is on Pebble, which is buried between the Pacific on one side and the Del

Monte forest on the other. It is a supreme test of golf, and I love to play it even when the weather isn't what you would consider ideal for golfer or gallery.

The wind kicked up on Sunday and was blowing fairly strong. It showed in the scores. My final round of 73 was one over par but I was mighty happy to settle for it. Only four of us finished under par for the tournament—Green, Tom Kite, Lou Graham, and I. When we started the final round there were eleven of us under par so you can see how wind conditions affect scoring.

A lot of scores soared into the 80s and there were even some triple bogeys by very fine golfers like Tom Watson, playing with me, who had two that last day.

I started the day with an eagle on two. That gave me a tremendous shot in the arm. I was a little concerned after the third hole when I three-putted for a bogey. On the next hole I drove into a bunker. Then I overshot the green into a pretty deep ravine, had trouble getting back, and finally one-putted for a six.

From 5 through 16 I shot even par, which was pretty good considering the conditions, and no one in the field could seem to make any substantial run at me. When the wind blows from your back at Pebble it is nearly impossible to keep the ball from going over the backside of the green. And when it blows in your face it makes it difficult to reach the greens.

It was a fine win and the $37,000 check made it even better. But what was most important, I proved to myself that I had truly come back, winning in a demanding test.

Anytime you can win the Crosby on those courses you are capable of winning any event in the world anytime you put everything together.

One of my cherished treasures from that triumph isn't very big but it is deeply appreciated.

Dear Gene:

Please accept my warmest congratulations on winning the Bing Crosby Tournament.

There are just no words to express my admiration of your tremendous courage, and to say the least, what a wonderful example I think you are.

May you go from strength to strength in all your endeavors in life.

Look forward to seeing you on the circuit.

Yours sincerely,

Gary Player

Sentiments like this from such a fine man and a marvelous golfer make the whole world wonderful. Such a letter is equal to any honor a man can possibly achieve.

Looking back on 1975, starting with the Crosby win, I feel the year has to rank with one of the best of my career, especially in light of my surgery.

Things didn't look too bright for a few months there. After winning the Crosby on January 26, there was a long spell of four months without any real shot at a triumph. Oh, I finished in a tie for ninth at Jackie Gleason Inverrary Classic at Lauderhill, Florida. Then I tied for seventh at the Tournament of Champions.

Then late in May at Danny Thomas's Memphis Classic I had one of the best four-round totals in my career. I shot rounds of 67–68–69–66 for a 270 total and that was 18 under par. I remember reading before the tournament that Gary Player had set a tourney record last year at 13 under par.

I was asked before the tournament what score I thought would win. Because I felt the course played a little tougher and the rough was deeper than the year before, I predicted no one would come close to what Gary shot in 1974. Then I shot five shots better. It was a fantastic total, really.

It's a long course, and when you can average 67.5 for four rounds of tournament golf you have your game pretty well in hand. I'd played in the Memphis tournament since 1958, and I'd come close many times, including a playoff or two. But I never took it all and never played this well.

I was very steady all around, but, what is really vital in any win, I putted just super, especially when I started out. And I've learned over the years if I start out well I usually play pretty well.

Memphis was almost a spectacular win for me since I was in the chase all the way and on the Colonial Country Club—when it's stretched out to 7,193 yards—they get a good run at you. It was my twenty-seventh career win on tour and a nice one to look back on, considering that I beat John Mahaffey by five strokes and Jack Nicklaus and Tom Weiskopf by seven.

I started out the final round the way we all would like to. I broke out of a tie with Mahaffey with a string of four straight birdies to begin the round. Some say that a seven-foot bird on fourteen won it for me, but I never chalk up a win until 18 and the field is in.

My third win was in the Westchester Classic and it was marked by both triumph and tragedy.

Like Memphis, I put together four fine rounds—68–68–69–66—and ended up after seventy-two holes in a tie with Julius Boros. It was another of those hot, humid, repressive eastern summer days and after we finished at 17 under par we went sudden death on the 15th hole—a par four dogleg of 470 yards.

Julie hit a pretty fair shot from the rough ending up just over the green. His chip came up short, where he putted about eight or ten feet past the cup. Then he missed his second putt and ended up with a double bogey—an unusual turn of events for Boros.

Now I had quite a bit of breathing room. I could two-putt the green and win. However, I slipped in a short putt of perhaps six feet to end it all right there on 15.

It was the twenty-eighth win of my career but I had a lot of thoughts about it even though it was worth $50,000.

I had really got into the playoff with Boros with a pair of eagles on that final eighteen. One of them was a hole in one on the 114-yard 14th with an eight-iron. I didn't have any thought of winning until I got the hole in one. It was the fifth one for me on tour and about the eleventh in my life.

I really didn't think I had too much of a chance then but

decided to give it all I had. It was 104 degrees—broiling —and I could see why Julius was sweltering. He weighs a lot more than I do and I was dripping.

It was almost as hot as the day in St. Louis when I won for the first time after surgery. But it wasn't just the heat that brought back memories of St. Louis. It was on Friday at Westchester that we got word that Gary Sanders had died in California of a melanoma similar to what I had.

The impact was vivid. You realize then how fortunate you are to be playing golf, to just be alive. When I hit that eight-iron for the hole in one I knew it was worth $8,000 to me. I decided right then that I would donate the money to Gary's memory. So when it was presented to me on the 18th green after the playoff, I signed it over to the American Cancer Society in the memory of Gary Sanders.

While you are happy in every triumph, this was quite tragic. Gary was only twenty-five, on the tour three years, and only a few weeks before I had spent a great deal of time telling him of my surgery. Now he was gone, leaving a lovely wife, Linda, a three-year-old daughter, and an infant daughter born after his death.

I kept thinking how fortunate I was to be at Westchester, to be playing golf and to win $50,000. And Gary was gone.

Three years before I didn't know if I was going to play any more golf. That's when you truly realize the full impact of cancer and how the good Lord has to be guiding you just a bit.

With Westchester being my third win of the year, I matched Nicklaus and Johnny Miller for 1975 tournament wins—pretty good company to be in—and it gave me the greatest earnings in sanctioned PGA play in my life. I ended up the year with $182,883. My previous best was in 1969 when I won $112,737.

As we had in 1974, we decided to wrap up the year in Tokyo in the Taiheiyo Masters (called the Pacific Masters by some). I was the halfway leader at 137 but then fell back to fourth behind Lee Elder after three rounds.

The final round on Sunday at Sohbu Country Club outside Tokyo was played in a worse rainstorm than the year before. It poured all day. It never let up. A lot of times we couldn't see where our drives went because of the low ceiling. You'd hit a drive and think it had gone down the fairway, but you wouldn't know for sure until you got down to where it finished.

Funny thing, the gallery was fairly large. If it had been an American tournament, in nine holes we'd have been rained out. But that course drained so well there was little standing water. It was wet around the edges but the greens were unbelievable even with the rain just coming down in sheets. We were all pretty soaked when it was over with.

I ended up the day with a one-under-par 70, to give me a 278, six under par for the tournament—a fine score considering the Sunday storm. Four tied at 279—Lee Elder, Hubert Green, Allen Miller, and Masashi Ozaki of Japan.

It was the second year running I had won the Pacific Masters and it was worth $65,000 for first place, plus another $500 for leading one round. When you couple that with my sanctioned earnings, 1975 was the greatest money year for me in my life at $248,383 total official money.

Reviewing the whole 1975 tour, I would have to say that while it may not have been my best year for total tournaments won, it surely enhanced my confidence. I feel now that I can play as well as ever, because anytime you can win the Crosby, Memphis, Westchester, and the Pacific Masters in one year you're capable of capturing any honor in golf.

There were a number of honors that had come my way after my surgery.

One I accepted with great pride because of the person for whom it was named. In 1973 I received the Bobby Jones Award for distinguished sportsmanship, awarded by the United States Golf Association. It was presented at the New York Biltmore but I couldn't be present since I was playing in the Crosby.

In 1974 I was inducted into the Golf Hall of Fame at a ceremony at the Allegheny Club at Three Rivers Stadium in Pittsburgh. Such awards are an honor and I do appreciate them, although I find it almost impossible to come up with adequate words to befit such occasions.

One award I particularly cherish came in 1973. It was the Ben Hogan Award, presented annually to a golfer who has overcome a handicap to play again. I felt tremendously honored to be named the recipient of the Hogan Award because I truly know what Ben Hogan overcame. I was there at Riviera in Los Angeles when he came back from his horrible auto crash and went into an 18-hole playoff only to lose to Sam Snead.

The Ben Hogan Award probably symbolizes best the reason all these words have been placed before you. It is awarded to a golfer "who overcame physical handicap, resuming the game, and serves as an inspiration."

It would do my heart good if, in some small way, I have been an inspiration to others.

Good luck and Godspeed.

Acknowledgments

To my wife Shirley, who diligently helped me reconstruct the little things of my life and whose attitude and cheerfulness all these years has meant so much, go my heartfelt thanks. To Jack Tobin, who spent so many hours turning our many, many hours of interviews into this story, my sincere appreciation.

To my mother, my brothers, my children, and my friends who helped substantiate facts that the years have dimmed in my memory go my thanks.

To Timothy P. Tobin, who transcribed the hours of tapes; to Patricia Fritz, public information secretary of the Tournament Players Division; and especially to the editorial team of Floyd Thatcher, vice president and executive editor of Words Books and Mrs. Pat Wienandt, the editor in charge, who carried forward the project from first fact to final edit, goes my grateful appreciation.

And finally to all of the golf world who have made all this possible—whether they be players, officials, caddies, spectators, or television fans—thank you from the bottom of my heart.

APPENDIX A

GENE ALEC LITTLER: TOURNAMENT HISTORY

(EVENTS IN TOP 10)

Date	Place	Event	Scores	Earnings
		1954		
1/21–24	1st	San Diego Open	67–66–69–72—274	Amateur
4/22–25	T5th	Tournament of Champions	69–68–76–76—289	$1,000.00
4/30–5/2	T4th	San Francisco Pro-Am	217	600.00
5/12–16	9th	Palm Beach Invitational	Minus 5	650.00
6/3–6	T5th	Western Open	72–73–66–70—281	833.33
6/17–19	2nd	U. S. Open	70–69–76–70—285	3,600.00
6/24–28	T7th	Insurance City Open	70–69–67–70—276	Probation
7/1–4	T2nd	Motor City Open	71–70–72–67—280	Probation
7/29–8/1	T2nd	Kansas City Open	70–67–65–68—270	1,950.00
8/5–8	2nd	All American Open	72–69–68–69—278	2,360.00
9/23–26	T6th	National Celebrities	69–66–75–72—282	1,500.00

Sanctioned earnings: $8,327. Place: 28th.

		1955		
1/6–9	1st	Los Angeles Open	72–67–68–69—276	$ 5,000.00
1/14–16	T6th	Bing Crosby Pro-Am	70–70–76—216	300.00

1/20-23	7th	San Diego Open	69-66-73-71—279	700.00
1/27-30	T8th	Thunderbird Invitational	67-69-71-67—274	309.00
2/3-6	1st	Phoenix Open	66-70-68-71—275	2,400.00
2/17-20	T3rd	Texas Open	67-67-64-71—269	996.67
3/3-6	T10th	Baton Rouge Open	71-69-72-71—283	288.75
3/21-22	T4th	Seminole Pro-Am	142	450.00
3/31-4/3	T6th	Azalea Open	68-71-70-69—278	643.34
4/28-5/1	1st	Tournament of Champions	69-71-68-72—280	10,000.00
5/19-22	T8th	Kansas City Open	68-71-71-70—280	710.00
5/26-29	T9th	Fort Wayne Invitational	68-69-73-71—281	404.00
6/1-5	T3rd	Palm Beach Pro-Am	62	650.00
6/1-5	4th	Palm Beach Low Pro	69	200.00
6/23-26	T3rd	Western Open	69-70-69-67—275	1,300.00
7/28-31	T9th	Rubber City Open	71-73-65-67—276	470.00
8/11-14	T3rd	World Championship	66-74-70-74—284	3,500.00
8/25-28	1st	Labatt Open	67-69-68-68—272	5,000.00
9/2-5	T6th	Insurance City Open	69-69-72-70—280	950.00
9/8-11	T3rd	Cavalcade of Golf	71-70-68-71—280	2,566.66
9/22-25	T7th	Carling Golf Classic	71-68-75-71—285	1,300.00

Sanctioned earnings: $28,974. Place: 5th.

1956

1/19-22	T5th	Caliente Open	70-72-70-73—285	$ 740.00
1/26-29	3rd	Palm Springs Invitational	66-76-69-66—277	750.00
2/2-5	4th	Phoenix Open	74-71-67-69—281	1,200.00

Date	Place	Event	Scores	Earnings
2/9-12	3rd	Tucson Open	68-66-69-65—268	1,000.00
2/16-19	1st	Texas Open	68-73-70-65—276	3,750.00
3/29-4/1	3rd	Azalea Open	66-70-69-71—276	1,170.00
4/26-29	1st	Tournament of Champions	70-71-69-71—281	10,000.00
5/17-20	T5th	Kansas City Open	70-70-71-67—278	1,666.67
6/1-4	T2nd	Texas International Open	64-66-67-70—267	5,778.50
6/7-10	1st	Palm Beach Invitational	Plus 55	3,000.00
6/28-7/1	T3rd	Insurance City Open	68-69-69-69—275	1,116.66
7/5-8	T6th	Canadian Open	71-70-68-70—279	750.00
8/16-19	2nd	Miller Open	64-69-70-66—269	4,000.00

Sanctioned earnings: $23,833. Place: 6th.

1957

Date	Place	Event	Scores	Earnings
3/14-17	T8th	St. Petersburg Open	66-71-72-71—280	$ 502.00
4/18-21	1st	Tournament of Champions	73-73-69-70—285	10,000.00
5/2-5	T7th	Colonial National	68-74-73-75—290	1,116.66
5/30-6/2	10th	Palm Beach Invitational	Minus 9	600.00
6/27-30	T2nd	Western Open	69-67-72-71—279	2,000.00
8/1-5	2nd	All American Open	72-71-71-63—277	2,300.00
8/8-11	T4th	World Championship	71-70-69-71—281	2,750.00
10/24-27	10th	Hesperia Open	68-69-75-71—283	600.00
11/2	T2nd	San Diego Pro-Am	65	237.50

Sanctioned earnings: $13,427. Place: 18th.

1958

Date	Place	Tournament	Scores	Earnings
1/17–20	T6th	Tijuana Open	71-71-68-72—282	$ 725.00
1/23–26	T2nd	Thunderbird Invitational	67-71-65-70—273	875.00
1/27	T10th	El Dorado Pro-Am	72	43.34
2/25	T1st	Port Arthur Pro-Am	67 (low pro)	270.00
2/25	T3rd	Port Arthur Pro-Am	60	90.00
4/24–27	T4th	Tournament of Champions	68-74-71-68—281	1,390.00
5/8–11	T9th	Arlington Hotel Open	71-67-71-71—280	732.50
5/22–25	T6th	Kansas City Open	73-71-66-68—278	916.67
6/4	T1st	Dallas Open Pro-Am	64 (low pro)	225.00
6/4	T3rd	Dallas Open Pro-Am	59	137.50
6/13–15	4th	U.S. Open	74-73-67-76—290	2,000.00
7/10–13	T8th	Insurance City Open	67-69-69-69—274	900.00
7/24–27	T7th	Eastern Open	73-72-67-72—284	875.00
8/28–30	T9th	Vancouver Open	69-69-74-67—279	1,250.00
8/28–30	T4th	Vancouver Pro-Am	68 (low pro)	102.50
9/18–21	2nd	Hesperia Open	67-62-72-71—272	1,500.00

Sanctioned earnings: $12,897. Place: 27th.

1959

Date	Place	Tournament	Scores	Earnings
1/15–18	T2nd	Bing Crosby National	73-67-70-71—281	$2,150.00
2/5–8	1st	Phoenix Open	67-63-67-71—268	2,400.00
2/12–15	1st	Tucson Open	65-67-68-66—266	2,000.00
2/19–22	T10th	Texas Open	76-72-67-69—284	690.00
2/27–3/1	T6th	Baton Rouge Open	70-70-71-76—287	650.00

Date	Place	Event	Scores	Earnings
3/6–9	T4th	New Orleans Open	73–64–72–75—284	1,100.00
3/20–23	T4th	St. Petersburg Open	72–70–72–68—282	900.00
4/2–5	T7th	Masters	72–75–72–71—290	1,740.00
4/23–26	3rd	Tournament of Champions	71–72–71–71—285	3,000.00
5/14–17	1st	Arlington Open	67–69–64–70—270	2,800.00
6/4–7	2nd	Eastern Open	65–67–71–71—274	1,900.00
6/25–28	3rd	Chicago Open	67–72–69–68—276	3,000.00
7/16–19	1st	Insurance City Open	64–66–72–70—272	3,500.00
7/30–8/2	10th	PGA	69–70–72–73—284	1,450.00
8/6–9	T2nd	Carling Open	71–64–70–72—277	2,050.00
8/27–30	1st	Miller Open	68–66–64–67—265	5,300.00
9/24–27	T10th	Golden Gate Championship	74–70–70–67—281	1,110.00
10/8–11	T10th	Hesperia Open	70–68–72–71—281	550.00
10/15–18	T8th	Orange City Open	68–70–68–72—278	625.00

Sanctioned earnings: $38,296. Place: 2nd.

1960

Date	Place	Event	Scores	Earnings
1/21–24	T6th	Bing Crosby National	67–73–71–80—291	$1,250.00
2/3–7	T9th	Palm Springs Classic	72–68–69–69–68—346	1,716.67
5/12–15	T2nd	Colonial National	69–70–70–72—281	2,500.00
5/26–29	T6th	500 Festival Open	67–70–68–70—275	1,760.00
6/1	1st	Memphis Pro-Am	64	300.00
6/2–5	T2nd	Memphis Open	74–70–65–64—273	2,500.00
6/9–12	1st	Oklahoma City Open	71–64–70–68—273	4,300.00

7/1–4	T4th	Buick Open	69-70-73-74—286	2,333.33
7/6–9	T9th	Canadian Open	68-68-68-77—281	875.00
7/14–17	T3rd	Western Open	73-69-68-69—279	1,750.00
7/28–31	1st	Eastern Open	65-68-73-67—273	3,500.00

Sanctioned earnings: $26,837. Place: 8th.

1961

4/13–16	T10th	Greater Greensboro Open	71-71-74-73—289	$ 800.00
5/11–14	T4th	Colonial National	72-70-67-75—284	1,900.00
6/1–4	T5th	Memphis Open	66-69-69-69—273	1,400.00
6/15–17	1st	U.S. Open	73-68-72-68—281	14,000.00
6/22–25	T7th	Western Open	69-74-68-67—278	1,056.66
7/27–30	T5th	PGA	71-70-72-69—282	2,208.33
8/10–13	T7th	Insurance City Open	70-68-67-70—275	1,250.00

Sanctioned earnings: $29,245. Place: 9th.

1962

1/25–28	1st	Lucky International	65-68-68-73—274	$ 9,000.00
1/31–2/4	T2nd	Palm Springs Classic	67-71-64-68-75—345	2,800.00
2/15–18	T3rd	Tucson Open	67-67-67-66—267	1,175.00
4/5–8	4th	Masters	71-68-71-72—282	6,000.00
4/26–29	T2nd	Texas Open	68-69-68-69—274	2,050.00

Date	Place	Event	Scores	Earnings
5/3–6	9th	Tournament of Champions	72–71–71–73—287	1,850.00
5/31–6/3	T2nd	Memphis Open	66–67–68–66—267	3,050.00
6/7–10	1st	Thunderbird Classic	67–71–70–67—275	25,000.00
6/14–16	T8th	USGA Open	69–74–72–75—290	1,766.67
8/2–5	T5th	Insurance City Open	68–66–71–68—273	1,600.00
8/9–12	T7th	American Golf Classic	72–71–73–71—287	1,800.00
8/23–26	T9th	Oklahoma City Open	69–72–74–74—289	1,100.00
8/31–9/3	T5th	Dallas Open	72–69–74–68—283	1,420.00
10/11–14	T10th	Bakersfield Open	69–70–69–74—282	1,200.00
10/25–28	T6th	Orange County Open	67–71–68–68—274	1,000.00

Sanctioned earnings: $66,200. Place: 2nd.

1963

Date	Place	Event	Scores	Earnings
1/4–7	T4th	Los Angeles Open	65–72–71–70—278	$2,120.00
1/30–2/3	T4th	Palm Springs Classic	70–73–72–68–64—347	2,450.00
2/14–17	T2nd	Tucson Open	69–70–69–69—277	2,050.00
3/21–24	T9th	Doral Open	70–71–73–77—291	1,400.00
3/28–31	T7th	Azalea Open	67–70–72–71—280	875.00
5/2–5	T8th	Tournament of Champions	73–74–68–69—284	1,850.00
5/9–12	T6th	Colonial National	74–71–69–73—287	2,200.00
5/23–27	T6th	Memphis Open	76–67–63–70—276	1,900.00
6/6–9	T5th	Buick Open	69–73–69–72—283	2,100.00
6/13–16	3rd	Thunderbird Classic	71–71–69–67—278	5,700.00

8/1-4	T8th	St. Paul Open	71-68-69-68—276	1,150.00
10/3-6	T7th	Whitemarsh Open	69-72-72-72—285	3,400.00

Sanctioned earnings: $32,566. Place: 12th.

1964

1/23-26	T5th	Lucky International	70-69-67-71—277	$2,450.00
2/6-9	T3rd	Phoenix Open	71-68-69-67—275	3,100.00
4/23-26	T4th	Texas Open	67-67-71-70—275	1,950.00
5/7-10	3rd	Colonial National	71-71-68-75—285	4,000.00
5/21-24	T4th	Memphis Open	66-69-66-71—272	2,216.66
5/27-31	T10th	"500" Festival Open	71-69-68-70—278	1,850.00
8/27-30	T8th	Carling Open	73-71-70-71—285	4,033.33

Sanctioned earnings: $33,173. Place: 15th.

1965

1/8-11	T9th	Los Angeles Open	73-69-73-69—284	$ 1,975.00
1/14-17	T9th	San Diego Open	62-70-71-71—274	1,200.00
4/8-11	T6th	Masters	71-74-67-74—286	3,800.00
5/6-11	T8th	Colonial National	69-71-73-69—282	2,850.00
5/13-16	T7th	New Orleans Open	65-73-69-70—277	3,200.00
6/17-20	T8th	USGA Open	73-71-73-72—289	2,500.00
6/24-27	T2nd	St. Paul Open	67-70-67-70—274	9,400.00
7/1-4	T4th	Western Open	69-69-73-64—275	3,066.67
7/14-17	1st	Canadian Open	70-68-69-66—273	20,000.00

Sanctioned earnings: $58,898. Place: 9th.

Date	Place	Event	Scores	Earnings
		1966		
2/10–14	3rd	Phoenix Open	70–71–69–70—280	$ 4,000.00
2/17–20	2nd	Tucson Open	71–71–68–68—278	5,000.00
4/28–5/1	T2nd	Texas Open	65–70–67–73—275	5,433.33
5/19–22	T7th	Colonial National	69–69–70–77—285	2,887.50
6/2–5	2nd	Memphis Open	66–66–66–72—270	12,000.00
7/21–24	T3rd	PGA	75–71–71–69—286	8,333.33
7/28–31	4th	"500" Festival	71–69–73–70—283	4,800.00
8/4–7	T8th	Cleveland Open	68–69–72–68—277	2,620.00
8/25–28	T3rd	Philadelphia Classic	71–68–71–71—281	6,100.00
10/20–23	3rd	Haig Mixed Foursome	72–73–68–67—280	2,250.00
10/27–30	4th	Hawaiian Open	72–69–70–65—276	3,150.00

Sanctioned earnings: $68,345. Place: 7th.

Date	Place	Event	Scores	Earnings
		1967		
3/30–4/2	6th	Greater Greensboro Open	70–70–68–67—275	$4,750.00
5/18–21	5th	Colonial National	71–73–68–71—283	4,945.00
6/29–7/2	T7th	Canadian Open	75–70–66–71—282	6,032.00
7/6–9	5th	"500" Festival	71–68–73–72—284	4,300.00
7/20–23	T7th	PGA	73–72–71–69—285	4,750.00
11/16–19	T10th	Haig Scotch Foursome	71–68–70–73—282	1,147.14

Sanctioned earnings: $38,086. Place: 32nd.

1968

1/18–21	Kaiser International	T3rd	71-70-66-69—276	$ 7,812.50
2/15–18	Phoenix Open	T7th	71-68-68-70—277	3,100.00
4/4–7	Greater Greensboro Open	T2nd	69-66-69-67—271	11,229.16
5/16–19	Colonial National	2nd	71-72-69-68—280	15,000.00
5/23–26	Memphis Open	T8th	73-67-65-67—272	2,620.00
10/31–11/3	Lucky International	T9th	72-69-67-68—276	2,400.00
11/7–10	Hawaiian Open	T8th	65-66-70-70—271	3,541.66

Sanctioned earnings: $61,631. Place: 26th.

1969

1/16–19	Kaiser International	T6th	69-70—139	$ 1,792.82
1/23–26	Bing Crosby National	T8th	73-74-70-72—289	2,901.43
1/30–2/2	San Diego Open	2nd	70-72-67-76—285	17,100.00
2/5–9	Bob Hope Classic	T5th	67-74-68-73-69—351	3,175.00
2/13–16	Phoenix Open	1st	69-66-62-66—263	20,000.00
2/20–23	Tucson Open	T4th	74-70-68-68—280	4,400.00
3/27–30	National Airlines	T7th	74-68-71-71—284	2,300.00
4/3–6	Greater Greensboro Open	1st	66-70-69-69—274	32,000.00
4/10–13	Masters	T5th	69-75-70-71—285	3,600.00
4/17–20	Tournament of Champions	4th	75-68-75-72—290	8,000.00
5/29–6/1	Memphis Open	T8th	65-69-69-70—273	2,812.50
6/26–29	Cleveland Open	T10th	71-73-71-67—282	1,045.00
7/3–6	Buick Open	T9th	70-72-70-75—287	1,812.50

Date	Place	Event	Scores	Earnings
7/24-27	T4th	American Classic	68-69-71-68—276	5,487.50
10/30-11/2	T7th	Kaiser International	74-68-69-69—280	1,450.00

Sanctioned earnings: $112,737. Place: 6th.

1970

Date	Place	Event	Scores	Earnings
1/15-18	T2nd	Phoenix Open	67-68-67-70—272	$ 9,556.25
2/4-8	T5th	Bob Hope Classic	72-69-72-70-66—349	4,870.84
4/9-12	2nd	Masters	69-70-70-70—279	17,500.00
5/14-17	T2nd	Colonial National	69-72-66-67—274	11,575.00
7/23-26	T5th	National Four Ball	69-65-65-64—263	3,650.00
8/13-16	T4th	PGA	72-71-69-70—282	8,800.00
10/22-25	T7th	Kaiser International	70-72-71-67—280	4,598.75

Sanctioned earnings: $79,001. Place: 22nd.

1971

Date	Place	Event	Scores	Earnings
4/8-11	T4th	Masters	72-69-73-69—283	$ 9,050.00
4/15-18	1st	Monsanto Open	71-67-71-67—276	30,000.00
4/22-25	5th	Tournament of Champions	72-71-74-71—288	6,770.00
5/20-23	1st	Colonial National	72-68-74-69—283	25,100.00
6/24-27	7th	Cleveland Open	66-68-70-68—272	4,800.00
8/25-29	T9th	U.S. Match Play	73-71-76—220	3,750.00

Sanctioned earnings: $98,687. Place: 14th.

1972

| 2/17-20 | T4th | Phoenix Open | 67-68-70-71—276 | $5,011.75 |

(Surgery performed April 4, 1972.)
Sanctioned earnings: $11,119. Place: 135th.

1973

1/11-14	T8th	Phoenix Open	69-69-64-69—271	$ 3,612.50
3/22-25	T10th	New Orleans Open	71-71-72-72—286	2,650.00
5/17-20	T4th	Memphis Open	71-73-70-71—285	6,492.60
6/21-24	7th	American Classic	72-69-66-71—278	5,120.00
7/19-22	1st	St. Louis Classic	66-66-68-68—268	42,000.00
8/2-5	T5th	Westchester Classic	68-69-71-66—274	9,433.33
8/16-19	T10th	U.S. Industries Classic	73-70-71-70—284	4,400.00

Sanctioned earnings: $95,308. Place: 18th.

1974

1/10-13	T6th	Phoenix Open	74-68-65-68—275	$ 5,100.00
1/17-20	T9th	Tucson Open	69-75-67-68—279	3,750.00
1/24-27	T2nd	San Diego Open	68-71-71-66—276	16,038.75
2/14-17	T10th	Los Angeles Open	71-69-72-73—285	3,450.00
2/21-24	T8th	Inverrary Classic	67-75-74-66—282	7,636.25
4/25-28	T5th	Tournament of Champions	70-69-75-71—285	8,133.34

Date	Place	Event	Scores	Earnings
6/27–30	T5th	Western Open	73–71–79–71—294	6,925.00
8/30–9/2	4th	Tournament Players	72–69–69–67—277	11,750.00
9/12–15	T6th	World Open	69–70–73–71—283	9,750.00
9/26–29	T7th	Kaiser International	69–71–72–70—282	4,612.50

Sanctioned earnings: $102,822. Place: 20th.
Earnings with Pacific Masters: $170,822.

1975

Date	Place	Event	Scores	Earnings
1/9–12	T7th	Phoenix Open	71–67–70–72—280	$ 4,095.00
1/23–26	1st	Crosby Pro-Am	68–71–68–73—280	38,410.00
2/27–3/2	T9th	Inverrary Classic	70–66–72–72—280	6,552.50
4/24–27	T7th	Tournament of Champions	69–72–74–70—285	6,667.50
5/22–25	1st	Memphis Classic	67–68–69–66—270	35,287.50
7/31–8/3	1st	Westchester Classic	68–68–69–66—271	50,000.00
8/7–10	T7th	U.S. PGA	76–71–66–71—284	6,917.50
10/2–5	T3rd	Kaiser International	65–70–69–72—276	9,275.00

Sanctioned earnings: $182,883. Place: 5th.
Earnings with Pacific Masters: $248,383.

APPENDIX B

Following are the leaders in total career winnings in sanctioned professional golf play. Through the 1975 season, eight players in the history of golf have earned over $1,000,000.

1.	Jack Nicklaus	$2,541,772.99
2.	Arnold Palmer	1,723,114.07
3.	Billy Casper	1,581,606.62
4.	Lee Trevino	1,398,651.94
5.	Bruce Crampton	1,323,400.33
6.	Tom Weiskopf	1,224,854.80
7.	Gene Littler	1,203,541.74
8.	Gary Player	1,163,153.49
9.	Miller Barber	994,869.00
10.	Julius Boros	993,756.10
11.	Frank Beard	951,596.54
12.	John Miller	947,152.59
13.	Dave Hill	922,233.87
14.	Bobby Nichols	906,277.55
15.	Dave Stockton	814,483.50
16.	George Archer	810,020.91
17.	Al Geiberger	794,505.90
18.	Dan Sikes, Jr.	773,508.66
19.	Doug Sanders	767,434.76
20.	Hale Irwin	760,055.93
21.	Tommy Aaron	745,708.77
22.	Gay Brewer	712,087.75
23.	Bob Murphy	708,392.47
24.	Ray Floyd	697,588.24
25.	Bert Yancey	688,124.85
26.	Charles Coody	663,253.39
27.	Bruce Devlin	660,455.78
28.	Don January	655,190.84
29.	Juan Rodriguez	650,970.65
30.	Bob Goalby	629,457.69

APPENDIX C

GOLF'S MILLIONAIRES: HOW THEY JOINED THIS VERY SELECT CIRCLE

Name	Date/Event/Position	Number of Events Entered	Wins	First Money Earned
Arnold Palmer	7/21/68 PGA Championship T2nd	368	52	5/29/55 Ft. Wayne Open T25th—$145
Billy Casper	1/11/70 Los Angeles Open Winner	297	43	6/26/55 Western Open T30th—$33.33
Jack Nicklaus	1/25/70 Bing Crosby Pro-Am 2nd	170	30	1/8/62 Los Angeles Open T50th—$33.33
Lee Trevino	5/20/73 Memphis Classic T2nd	176	15	6/20/66 U.S. Open T54th—$600
Bruce Crampton	7/1/73 Western Open T4th	420	14	2/25/57 Houston Open T13th—$693.75
Jack Nicklaus*	12/1/73 Disney World Winner	76	21	1/25/70 Bing Crosby 2nd—$11,840.83

Gary Player	4/14/74 Masters Winner	269	17	3/31/57 Azalea Open T25th—$16.16
Tom Weiskopf	8/25/74 Westchester Classic 3rd	250	9	8/9/64 Western Open T30th—$487.50
Gene Littler	9/1/74 Tournament Players 4th	487	25	8/1/54 Kansas City Open T2nd—$1,950.00

*On December 1, 1973, Jack Nicklaus achieved his second million dollars in tournament play, the fastest that amount has ever been won, both in length of time and in number of tournaments entered.

APPENDIX D

Official List of 1975's 60 Leading Money-Winners

These players are exempt from having to play a qualifying round to enter PGA tournament events.

1. Jack Nicklaus	$298,149	
2. Johnny Miller	226,118	
3. Tom Weiskopf	219,140	
4. Hale Irwin	205,380	
5. Gene Littler	182,883	
6. Al Geiberger	175,693	
7. Tom Watson	153,795	
8. John Mahaffey	141,471	
9. Lee Trevino	134,206	
10. Bruce Crampton	132,532	
11. Bob Murphy	127,471	
12. Hubert Green	113,569	
13. Ray Floyd	103,627	
14. Billy Casper	102,275	
15. Lou Graham	96,425	
16. Jerry McGee	93,569	
17. J. C. Snead	91,822	
18. Tom Kite	87,045	
19. Charles Coody	86,812	
20. Pat Fitzsimons	86,181	
21. Miller Barber	81,993	

31. Gary Groh	$68,296	
32. Ben Crenshaw	63,528	
33. Brian Allin	60,326	
34. Peter Oosterhuis	59,935	
35. Rod Curl	59,599	
36. Arnold Palmer	59,017	
37. Don Iverson	56,559	
38. Gibby Gilbert	56,279	
39. Eddie Pearce	54,595	
40. Larry Ziegler	54,265	
41. Joe Inman, Jr.	53,225	
42. Bob Wynn	52,414	
43. Forrest Fezler	52,157	
44. David Graham	51,642	
45. Jim Colbert	50,111	
46. Bobby Nichols	49,835	
47. Mark Hayes	49,297	
48. Leonard Thompson	48,748	
49. Ron Funseth	48,453	
50. Jim Simons	47,724	
51. Ed Sneed	46,634	

22. Jerry Heard	81,687
23. Roger Maltbie	81,035
24. Dave Hill	80,533
25. Rik Massengale	77,079
26. B. R.(Mac)McLendon	76,971
27. Gary Player	73,943
28. Dave Stockton	72,885
29. Don Bies	69,968
30. Don January	69,034

52. Tom Jenkins	45,267
53. Andy North	44,729
54. Bob E. Smith	44,720
55. Steve Melnyk	44,707
56. John Schlee	44,337
57. Wally Armstrong	44,078
58. Art Wall	43,589
59. Gary McCord	43,028
60. Gil Morgan	42,772